The Boys from Boston

The Boys from Boston

———

Gary Cullen

ISBN: 0692499903
ISBN 13: 9780692499900
Library of Congress Control Number: 2016900501
Gary Cullen, Vallejo, CA

"The Second World War transformed the city of Vallejo like no other event in it history. Thousands of men and women, both military and civilian, flocked to Vallejo to aid in the war effort, but none made a greater impact than the "Boys from Boston." Gary Cullen's thorough and well-researched history of the 211th Anti-Aircraft Coast Artillery tells the story of the important contributions made by these "boys." While they helped defend our nation, the men of the 211th also made a long-lasting impact on the community as a whole."

James Kern
Executive Director
The Vallejo Naval & Historical Museum

"Gary Cullen has done a lot of good things with his new book, "The Boys from Boston." He has related the fascinating World War II story of some 1,800 men in the 211th Anti-aircraft Artillery Unit from Boston, Massachusetts, who at the last minute got orders to guard Vallejo rather than board transport ships bound for combat zones in the Pacific Theater. Gary has described how the "Boys from Boston" were welcomed with open arms by Vallejoans and how, after the war, about 300 of the men in their unit decided to stay in California or, after going home to the East Coast for awhile, returned to the West Coast. Many of the men in the unit came straight back to Vallejo. They married, raised families and contributed in many significant ways to the town. Thanks, Gary, for telling this story of such a positive development that emerged from the chaos of war. Had the trains transporting the "Boys" not been delayed by railroad track damage in a remote area of Arizona, they might have made it to those military transport ships and never seen the town that became their new home."

Brendan Riley
Vallejo Heritage Society

Table of Contents

Prologue

The 211th Coast Artillery (A.A.)

First Corps of Cadets

THE FIRST CORPS of Cadets of Massachusetts is one of the oldest military organizations in the United States, with an ancestry that can be traced back to 1741. Its motto is Monstrat Viam — "It Points the Way."

The "Independent Company of Cadets" first served as the bodyguard of the royal governors of the Province of Massachusetts Bay.

John Hancock, who later became governor of Massachusetts, would serve as a Colonel in the Corps in 1774. In 1777, the Corps reorganized under the command of Colonel Henry Jackson, forming Jackson's Continental Army. The Corps would later be designated the First American Regiment of Infantry in 1784, becoming the last regiment of the Continental Army to be mustered out of service and, thus, the direct precursor of the First Regiment of the regular Army organized under the Constitution of the United States in 1789.

In March 1922, the Corps became the 211th Machine Gun Battalion, Coast Artillery Corps, but in May 1923 was reorganized again as the 2nd Battalion, 211th Artillery, Coast Artillery Corps.

The Corps was later reorganized again as a two-battalion regiment in June 1926 as the 211th Coast Artillery Regiment. The 211th was actually an anti-aircraft artillery regiment but assigned to the Coast Artillery, which had the mission of providing both coast and anti-aircraft artillery units. With the Corps' new mission of anti-aircraft artillery, it turned its attention toward recruiting and training for its federal mission. No longer was the Corps an exclusive social organization.

Intelligent, educated young men were invited to join. Unlike other National Guard units, however, prospective recruits had to be sponsored by a current member and were interviewed by a special committee before final acceptance into the Corps.

Not all applicants were accepted. Drill pay was turned in to the unit fund to support the many social, athletic and ceremonial activities of the Corps.

The Corps also reorganized its regimental band, which played at monthly dances. Drill and ceremonies were still an important part of the Corps' activities. A regimental parade was held every month, and the Governor would review the Corps each year. The only dress uniform was the Army issue Class A olive drab uniform with a choke collar, later changed to a roll collar with tie.

Drills were held once a week. Annual training was 15 days, with initial summer camps held at coast artillery installations such as Fort Wright and Fort Terry, then later at Camp Edwards, Massachusetts. The Corps was noted for its esprit de corps and spit and polish. The Corps' drill team competed in national drill competitions in full dress uniform. Athletics were very important and the Corps' teams attracted some of Boston's finest athletes. The 211th fielded baseball, football, track, pistol and rifle teams, as well as a platoon of boxers. The biggest football game of the year was between the 211th and the 101st Engineers and was played at Harvard Stadium.

During World I, the Cadets became the 101st Engineering Regiment, American Expeditionary Force, and served with distinction in France, where they saw heavy action. Meanwhile, the Veteran Association requested a State Guard Unit be formed to carry on at home. They were very active in helping to preserve order during the Boston Police strike of 1919.

In September 1940, the 211th Coast Artillery Anti-Aircraft Corps became one of the first units to be called to active duty in anticipation of American involvement in World War II. The 211th saw no overseas action as a unit during World War II but, instead, furnished many officers and enlisted men to other units, which served in all theaters and campaigns.

The 211th was alerted for overseas movement to the Pacific in the fall of 1941. However, due to a possible act of sabotage which caused their train to be derailed, their order to move west to the Pacific was cancelled. Instead, the regiment received orders to immediately move to Mare Island Naval Shipyard and Vallejo, California. The 211th would leave Camp Hulen, Texas on

December 9 by train, and arrive in Vallejo on December 14.

Under threat of a further Japanese air attack following Pearl Harbor, the 211th occupied hastily built battery positions to provide 24-hour air defense for Mare Island and Vallejo. The Corps' strength at the time was over 1,800 men. (1)

CHAPTER 1

The Early Years

*"All were young men between the
ages of 18 and 24.
All wanted to serve their
country."*

THE GOOD TIMES of the 1920's came to an end
in Boston, as in other parts of the United
States, during the Great Depression of the
1930's. Business declined, and many compa-
nies and industries even went broke.

In the 1930's, American capitalism practically stopped working. For more than a
decade, from 1929 to 1940, America's free-
market economy failed to operate at a level that allowed most Bostonians to attain
economic success. With the onset of World
War II pending, the complex problems of
Boston politics were obscured by the urgency of national survival. With a growing
deficit, an unbalanced budget, dishearten-
ing high taxes, an inability to attract government funding or corporate investments,
and a constant state of warfare between

1

the Irish-Catholic political system and the Yankee-Protestant financial establishment, Boston was in trouble. The economic collapse was terrifying in its scope and impact. By 1933, the average Boston family income had tumbled 40 percent, from $2,300 in 1929 to just $1,500.   The unemployment rate in Boston in 1939 was 17.2%. Communities were still struggling to recover from the Great Depression. (2)

In late 1939, a full two years before the United States would enter World War II, President Franklin Roosevelt decided it was time to invest time and money into our country's defense. Despite his promise to keep the nation out of the war in Europe, Roosevelt carefully and deliberately prepared the country for a worst-case scenario. By the spring of 1940, he convinced Congress to increase defense spending, enlarge the army, and expand the U.S. military air force. Through billions of dollars in federal spending, largely focused on rearmament and national security, Roosevelt managed to funnel money into a peacetime draft, increase wages for military personnel, offer subsidies for defense manufacturing, and grant loans to aid Great Britain and the Soviet Union. When the Japanese attacked Pearl Harbor in December 1941, the nation would be ready.

The Boys who would make up the 211th came from various parts of Massachusetts. They were made up of many ethnicities, but mostly Irish, Italian and Portuguese. Most were Roman Catholic. All were young men between the ages of 18 and 24. All wanted to serve their country.

Their families were struggling to survive and money was tight. They had grown up during the Depression era and had seen poverty close-up. Thus, enlisting in the Army was looking pretty darn good for the Boys. Patriotism may have played a big part in their enthusiasm, but economics was the true motivating factor. While making $25 a month for serving as a soldier part-time and wearing their new crisp uniforms seemed attractive, few of them thought of the possibility of going off to war. Why should they worry? Little did the Boys know what lay ahead. But President Roosevelt did.

Training

*"For they've done their hitch in
hell."*

UNTIL THE CALL came on that fateful day of
December 7, 1941, it was all about training
for the Boys from Boston. Their first stop
was Camp Edwards in Falmouth, Massachusetts
for basic training.   For most, it was the
first formal indoctrination into service.
The Boys hailed from all parts of the state
to become over 1000 strong, and came thinking they would do their 30 days and then
return to civilian life knowing that they
would be ready to serve if called into
action.

Prior to going to Camp Edwards, the
Boys who had enlisted into the Guard earlier were accustomed to putting on uniforms two Sundays a month and reporting to
the National Guard Armory at the Wentworth
Institute in Boston for routine training.
That was about to change.

After completion of their physical exams, the Boys spent that first week setting up tents and equipment at their Guard encampment near Cape Cod, Massachusetts. As new soldiers in training, the boys were quickly drilled on the fundamentals of basic training, organizational skills, equipment review, living in the field, using camouflage and, basically, learning to become a fighting unit.

The Boys were issued the standard field equipment of a blanket roll, one woolen uniform, two woolen shirts, four pairs of socks, four suits of underwear, one pair of shoes, a campaign hat, a mess kit, toilet articles, a rifle, a cartridge belt, a helmet, an overcoat, puttees and a bayonet.

During their stay, they worked on physical development. The initial training for the new recruits was pretty tough. Millions of men were being called up to fight in World War II, and not all of them were prepared for the rigors of combat. To get the Boys in fighting shape, the Army had implemented a systematic physical development program as part of the Combat Basic Training course. The Army Ground Forces Test was designed to assess whether the program was having its desired effect. The test included squat jumps, sit-ups, pull-ups, push-ups and a 300-yard run. The emphasis was on functional fitness and giving the Boys the strength, mobility and endurance they would need to tackle real tasks on the battlefield. Therefore, the new objective of physical screening for future enlistees was to eliminate the physically and mentally unfit who would not be capable of performing a military function, and also to eliminate those who might reasonably be expected to break down while on active duty. This would provide an Army most likely to withstand the rigors of service and would also avoid inducting men who might shortly be discharged, and, therefore, be eligible for disability payments and hospital expenses from the government. The Boys from Boston would pass with flying colors. Ultimately, the goal of this intensive training was the expectation that each outfit would become a crack anti-aircraft unit, armed with the newest weapons and trained in their usage. (3)

Soon after the Boys got settled into their daily routine at Camp Edwards, word leaked out that they would be relocating to Camp Hulen, in Palacios, Texas. A few days later, they received the official news that President Roosevelt truly did have other plans for them. On September 16, 1940, the 211th, with Colonel Stuart G. Hall commanding, would became one of the first National Guard Regiments inducted into active service. (See Executive Order 8530)

Their service was scheduled to last for a period of 12 months. After hearing the order that they were going active, they were told they had ten days to get their personal affairs in order.

On that tenth day, the Boys spent their last hours in their tent city/encampment watching it magically disappear as they disassembled their gear in preparation for loading it onto the trucks that would shuttle it across camp to the waiting freight cars.

They would spend their last night in hastily erected two storied barracks, which were rushed into place to house the boys during their final night. Small groups of the Boys were given leave after evening mess with the instruction to return by taps.

There were a few extreme exhibitions of emotions, as the Boys prepared to meet their loved ones for the last few minutes before boarding the trains that would carry them south. It was a day of great activity for the entire outfit, enhanced by the thousands of visitors who came to wish them a safe journey.

The Boys could be seen spending the last few precious moments with their loved ones. The chilling affect of the near freezing weather was contrasted on all sides by the warmth of these moments.

That evening, Colonel Hall received notification from his junior officers that the

Boys were ready to go. They departed the following morning for Camp Hulen.

The first train was scheduled to leave at 0815 and was under the command of Captain Bohlin. It was to carry HQ Battery, Battery C, H and Medical. The second train under the command of Captain Marquis, would depart at 1015, with Battery A and F onboard. Major Sweeney was to command the third train with Batteries B and G, and the entire 211th band on board. They were scheduled to depart at 1215.

Finally, the last of the Regiment, with Colonel Hall's oversight, would depart at 1415. Battery D and E were on board. All the trains would have dozens of flat cars weighed down with trucks and their anti-aircraft guns. (4)

All the Boys were read the Articles of War/Code of Conduct, while waiting for their trains to roll. It would take the trains several days to reach Camp Hulen. They traveled through the towns of Harrisburg and Altoona, stopping at each just enough to disembark and to stretch and limber up. They would continue though the cities of Indianapolis and St. Louis, with the first of the four trains arriving in the latter at 1700. Most of the Boys were again allowed to detrain with instructions to be back on board within the hour. Some of the Boys quickly broke out some gloves and balls, and a few pickup games of catch were played in the hour before reloading. Travel continued through Little Rock and Texarkana. In Texarkana, the Boys were allowed to parade through the city streets and were greeted by the locals. During the parade, the 211th quartermasters spent their time quickly gathering up additional supplies from the town stores.

While the Boys rode the trains, other anti-aircraft regiments from other parts of the northeast traveled by motorcade enroute to the Texas camp. The motorcades created a spectacle of their own as they passed through the towns. The usual motorcades were made up of over three hundred vehicles of all sizes and types, and were a showcase of the latest in mobile anti-aircraft equipment. It created quite a bit of excitement for the local citizens as the display of soldiers and modern equipment paraded through town after town. (5)

Camp Edwards would continue to function as a sending off point for later troops, as well as a training ground for future anti-aircraft units. The camp continued to function this way until the war ended.

Camp Hulen Poem
1941
(Author Unknown)

I'm sitting here thinking
of the things I left behind
And I hate to put on paper
What's running through my mind
We've dug a million ditches
And cleared ten miles of ground
And a meaner place this side of hell
Is waiting to be found
But this one consolation
Gather closely while I tell
When we die we go to heaven
For we've done our hitch in hell

Washed a million dishes
Peeled a million spuds
Rolled a million blanket rolls
And washed the captain's duds
The number of parades we've stood
Is very hard to tell
We won't have to parade in heaven
For we've done it here in hell

We've killed a million snakes and bugs
That cried out for our oats
And shook a million pounds of sand
Out of our many coats
We've marched a million miles
And made a million camps

So when our work on earth is done
Our friends behind will tell
When they died they went to heaven
For they've done their hitch in hell

When taps are finally sounded
And we lay away our troubles and cares
We will do our last parade
Up those shining, golden stairs
The angels all will welcome us
And the harps will start to play
It is then that we will hear St. Peter yell-
"Take front seats boys"
For you have done your hitch in Hell!

On October 25, 1940, the first train of Boys arrived in Camp Hulen at 0630, and was greeted with a downpour of rain. The camp's 1,400 plus acres, at best, were a wasteland of mud. Years later, Bill Pendergast described Camp Hulen as a "deserted and decrepit wasteland surrounded by swamp-water." The relics of the old WWI camp still stood, mostly in the form of old wooden framed tent-barracks, that had become the homes of rattlers, scorpions and other infestations.

The rains continued as the trains started to unload. The construction teams, made up of civilian contractors and members of the Work Projects Administration, had arrived earlier to help rebuild the old barracks. They were running in high gear, battling their biggest deterrent of navigating the mud of the camp and the surrounding areas. The torrential downpours made life so miserable for the Boys that they dubbed it "Lake Hulen" and "Swamp Hulen."

The seas of mud would hinder, but not stop, the work being done to prepare the camp. Pictures of the lakes of water and mud had been sent to Washington, causing concerns about delays in the construction, thus, causing a delay in the critical training ordered by the National Defense Program.

The engineers knew thousands of additional troops would be arriving over the next six months, and their duty was to complete this project on time. The fears proved groundless as their work progressed according to schedule. The work included in the original program called for an expenditure of $2 million, with the expectation that it would be completed by December 1, 1941. This expectation just reinforced the theory that the "powers that be" in Washington knew the Boys were going to war. (6)

During the construction phase, the huts being built for the Boys were to be 14 x 14 feet in size. They were made of plywood on the outside, with exposed 2 x 4 lumber showing on the inside, and to the Boys they looked like a good wind would blow them away. They had no insulation, inside finishing or even a coat of paint. One of the Boys was overheard saying, "I've been in a lot of outhouses but this is the first time I'm gonna sleep in one." The upper part of the hut was screened in and there were awnings made of plywood sheets that could be lowered over the screening during a rainstorm. Inside, there was a wooden floor, a potbelly stove and canvas cots with wooden frames. Each cot had a 3" thick mattress. Each hut slept six men.

The Boys in front of their hut.

The rain continued to fall and Camp Hulen eventually became buried in an adobe-type mudpack. This period was very trying, not only for the soldiers, but also for the carpenters, plumbers and electricians, thousands of whom toiled around the clock in eight hour shifts through the downpours to build the new latrines, mess-halls and warehouses. The buildings sprang up like fast growing grain. The new water and gas line ditches crisscrossed the area, causing an unforeseen draining of the water, which actually helped the flooding streets.

211th member Ed Rollins (2nd from left) leading his crew.

The Boys plodded through the slippery areas of the camp, never knowing when an innocent looking puddle might actually be a deep hazard waiting to be stepped in. Even with the elements, the Boys took it all in stride, bantering among themselves and trying to keep their positive attitudes, knowing that it had to dry up at some point. Thousands of tons of crushed seashells were bought into the camp and laid onto the muddy streets to improve traction and traffic. By December, the sun was starting to shine fairly regularly and combined with the balmy gulf breezes, the mud-shell mixture started to harden.

The recently constructed dining halls were now serving meals around-the-clock, catering to the hard working civilians and soldiers. The Boys were so delighted to no longer have to take their mess kits to the portable field kitchens that many could be seen dancing all the way to the dining halls.

The Boys dancing to the Dining Hall.

The construction program had been underway for over four months when the Boys finally started to see the resemblance to what appeared to be a carefully developed and well-ordered military community.

When completed, Camp Hulen boasted 400 semi-permanent buildings, 2,285 framed and screened tents, guest housing, a 500 bed hospital, a dental clinic, a fire station, warehouses, a cold storage plant, a sewage disposal plant, incinerators, service laundries, a bakery, a post office, a library, a service club, a theater, five recreation halls and a host of other amenities. (7)

Camp Hulen 1940

The hospital alone was made up of 38 buildings overlooking the bay at the southern end of the camp. Each ward of the hospital came with its own solarium.

The warehouses were all built in a fashion that allowed the trains to roll up to the sides, permitting a quick and easy loading and unloading of supplies to insure maximum efficiency. A 10 foot non-climbable fence with floodlight towers was installed around the entire camp.

After awhile, mail started to arrive at the camp, and there wasn't any bigger morale booster for the Boys. The mail would arrive almost weekly and was delivered to the individual batteries. Its delivery and distribution at mail call caused a friendly jostling between the Boys trying to get into position. They would come early and stay until their names were called.

The Boys waiting for mail call.

The Boys were happy. Their minds had relaxed, and their bodies had hardened. They realized that with at least eight more months of intensive training before them, they now had the self-confidence to meet the future.

Brigadier General Harvey C. Allen, who took over the command of the camp in 1940, commented on the completion of the construction, *"The courage, determination, and initiative that has been displayed by all ranks during the adverse and trying conditions that have existed at times during the inclement weather with the resultant mud and water has been most commendable. The willingness with which all the ranks have accepted these conditions is indicative of the highest morale and fine military qualities of the troops in this command. It is an honor and privilege to serve with the units at this station."*

While at Camp Hulen, the Boys' primary purpose was to be trained in the operation and usage of anti-aircraft artillery. A wide variety of anti-aircraft artillery weaponry existed during World War II at the time, but the Boys would focus on the usage of multiple-mounted .50-caliber machine guns and 90mm AA guns M1.

The .50 caliber machine gun had an effective firing range of approximately 2,000 yards, but could shoot to a distance of nearly 7,400 yards, and had a rate of fire of approximately 1000 rounds per minute.

The 90 mm (3.5") in caliber had a 15-foot barrel and was capable of firing a 90x600 mm shell approximately 58,474 feet horizontally, or at a maximum altitude of 34,060 feet. It had the capability of firing 25 rounds per minute. It would be the Army's primary anti-aircraft gun until it was replaced by guided missile systems in the 1950's.

The Boys posing for the camera
during a training session.

It wasn't "all work and no play" however. Because of the influx of over 10,000 military and 2,000 civilian workers, a major impact was felt on the town of Palacios. (5)

Its population soared almost overnight from 2,281 to nearly 15,000. The town's urban growth was visibly transformed in every way possible; physically, socially and economically. The locals could not have predicted such growth. There was an immediate housing shortage with people living in their cars and using the restrooms of the four gas stations in town. Temporary tent housing popped up on every vacant lot in town. Trailers without plumbing were scattered about the town. Temporary business shacks went up overnight beside the established business houses, creating real fire and safety hazards, as well as giving the downtown area an unsightly appearance.

The increase of the male population also led to an increase in prostitutes. The prostitutes could be seen walking the streets, and soliciting the soldiers was a fairly common sight. The local officials were concerned about this new health issue, but were unable to curb prostitution, and soon became overburdened by the amount of work required of them to keep their community safe. They eventually partnered with the Palacios Chamber of Commerce, the U.S. Provost Marshall, the Army Medical Officers and surrounding medical organizations to address the problem. The soldiers were educated on the risks of dating the "ladies of the evening" and how to take precautions when engaging in those activities.

The Army also found other ways to distract the Boys. An extensive athletic program was initiated at the Camp, which included baseball, softball, field hockey and basketball intramural programs. Saturday nights were chosen for round-robin basketball tourneys, using the high-school gyms in the towns of Palacios and nearby Wharton as places to play.

Keeping with the tradition of the Corps of Cadets, some of the Boys built a professional-like boxing ring for the local leather pushers, added rails for gymnastics, and laid down wooden floors for a tennis court and weight room.

The Boys were also greeted with the good news that the local community wanted to honor them by hosting a military ball. The entire 211th Regiment Band was invited to play, and Colonel Hall made every effort to accommodate as many of the Boys as possible. The ball provided the first real break in the military routine since their arrival to camp, and also gave those Boys lucky enough to attend the opportunity to dress up in their formal wear for the first time since arriving at Camp Hulen.

The 211th Band was largely responsible for the success of the ball. Under the direction of Private Joe Toronto, an experienced trumpeter, the band practiced for several weeks before the ball to prepare for the occasion. They were so successful that their dance band received praise from everyone in attendance. Throughout the dance, the Boys broke out in spontaneous versions of southern songs, including "Old Man River," among others; the band also played a large mix of "Big Band" songs, being broken up by an occasional "Paul Jones" dance, where dance partners were changed frequently, which allowed a good mix of merriment and camaraderie.

When the music finally stopped at midnight, the Boys were ready to return to camp, sleepy but hoping to return again for some more of the great southern hospitality to which they had just been treated.

———

Louisiana Maneuvers

"We traded the poisonous centipedes and rattlesnakes of Texas for the dangerous coral snakes and scorpions of Louisiana."

STAFF SERGEANT LEO CULLEN

In the summer of 1942, the Boys received orders that they were moving again, this time to Louisiana for additional training, training that would be recorded in the history books as the Louisiana Maneuvers.

Years later, some of the Boys would joke about the maneuvers, stating that there just wasn't enough equipment to go around. These situations were really far and few when one considered the historical significance of these maneuvers. The Louisiana Maneuvers could be measured in two ways. First, the enormity of the numbers, with over 500,000 soldiers involved, and secondly, the presence of such Army officers as Major General George Patton, General Walter Krueger, Colonel Dwight Eisenhower, and the Army's top General and Chief of Staff, General Omar Bradley.

The maneuvers were referred to as the "Big One" because of the number of soldiers and the large amount of Louisiana land used as the arena for the mock battle. When all was said and done, senior officers for the assembly had mapped out more than 3400 square miles to be used as battlefields. (see map)

The maneuvers were to serve as a trial run for battles between two armies and were judged by the top brass. General George Marshall said before the end of the exercise, "I want the mistakes made down in Louisiana, not over in Europe. If it *doesn't work, find out what we need to make it work."*

The maneuvers were meant to be challenging and instructive. The military worked tirelessly to devise a series of increasingly demanding tests that would prepare soldiers for the battlefield and test command arrangements from the squad level to full army level. Marshall wanted to test units under as many different conditions as possible to see whether they could communicate with each other, deploy according to schedules and, perhaps most importantly, cover long distances at night. The exercises were designed to be exhaustive. There would be limited sleep on a real battlefield, thus, there would be little time for relaxation in Texas and Louisiana.

A week before the maneuvers were scheduled to begin, a hurricane struck Louisiana. Rains flooded the area and rivers were swollen with water. The trucks became stuck in the mud and roads became practically impassable. Patton's observation of the maneuver resulted in his statement, *"If you could take these trucks through Louisiana, you could take them through hell."* Some of the Boys were already thinking that rain and mud were becoming a routine occurrence in their daily lives and questioned whether hell would even come close in comparison.

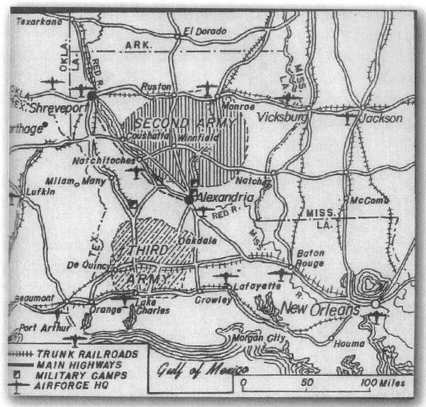

Louisiana Maneuvers Map

The 2nd and 3rd Armies battled each other for two weeks, and were identified as Red Army and Blue Army. General Ben Lear commanded the "Red" Army, with General Walter Krueger commanding the "Blue". The 211th was assigned to the Blue Army.

In the first phase of training scheduled from September 15-20, 1941, Krueger quickly proved himself to be the more modern general. He responded skillfully to a changed battle situation by re-orienting his front from northeast to northwest, and was able to inflict a series of reverses on Lear's forces. In the second phase, which ran from September 24-28, 1941, Krueger continued to have the superior force, and was able to advance on Lear's forces.

The maneuvers also allowed the 211th, along with all the other AA regiments, to fine-tune their readiness skills. The ideal mobile artillery regiment was one so organized and trained that at a moment's notice, soldiers would pack all equipment and personnel onto their 40 trucks and be ready to go into the field.

Col. Hall with staff going over strategy.

Under war strength, a battery consisted of approximately 174 men. These men would be required to take with them all things required to engage in a battle for an extended period of time. In addition to the anti-aircraft artillery, they packed clothing, food and shelter to sustain them for whatever time period required.

In modern war, no army can afford to risk "living off the land" as did armies in the past. And because of the speed with which things could happen in mechanized warfare, no individual soldier could depend on remaining close to his source of supplies.

Consequently, each soldier was required to carry on his back the necessities of life. Each soldier, in addition, was responsible for his part of the war equipment of his battery. This included ammunition, tools and communications gear.

A non-commissioned officer was assigned to each battery truck and was to follow the instructions of the battery's four commissioned officers as to on- loading their trucks with the allotted supplies. It was the non-com's responsibility to know every piece of equipment that was to go onto his truck, and to make sure that all was loaded. There is not a time during war to wonder whether you remembered to bring something vital. And in a war, there's no chance for second-guessing.

At 1645 on September 28, 1941 the troops were told that the "war" was over, and that the non-coms could start preparing their trucks for their long convoy back to Camp Hulen.

The 211th was notified that the senior officers were highly pleased with their performance. Each Boy was given three cans of beer apiece in celebration of his successful participation in the maneuvers.

Within three days, the entire 211th had returned to Camp Hulen, and would spend the next week unpacking, cleaning and restocking the trucks and other gear. There was a sense of pride and accomplishment that could be felt thoughout the regiment. The Boys felt they were ready if and when they would be called upon to fight a real war.

Camp Hulen would continue to be used as a Coast Artillery Anti-Aircraft training site, even after the declaration of war. In the interest of national security, very little information was made available to the public as to what was going on in the camp. Due to the anti-aircraft training, most of the waters in the area were included in the "Danger Zone Regulations." No boats were permitted to enter the restricted area from 0800 to 1800 on weekdays without obtaining clearance from military officials.

AA Units with their guns pointing
towards the Danger Zone.

On February 15, 1943, part of the camp was established as an independent prisoner of war camp to house up to 250 German POW's. Later, in January 1944, the entire camp was converted to a POW camp, with the Germans who were housed there being farmed out to help with agricultural work in the county. On May 31, 1946, the War Department declared Camp Hulen surplus and returned it to the Texas National Guard. Rather than use it for summer training, the guard slowly dismantled it for scrap. In 1965, the

site was sold to developers hoping to con-
struct an industrial park.   The army air
base later became the Palacios Municipal
Airport.

CHAPTER 3

Executive Order 8530

August 31, 1940

BY VIRTUE OF the authority conferred upon me by Public Resolution No. 96, 76th Congress, approved August 27, 1940, and National Defense Act of June 3, 1916, as amended, and as Commander-in-Chief of the Army and Navy of the United States, I hereby order into the active military services of the United States, effective September 16, 1940, the following units and members of the National Guard of the United States to serve in active military service of the United States for a period of twelve consecutive months, unless sooner relieved:

UNITS
All active elements of:
44th Division
30th Division
45th Division
41st Division

197th Coast Artillery (Anti-Aircraft)
198th Coast Artillery (Anti-Aircraft)
202nd Coast Artillery (Anti-Aircraft)
203rd Coast Artillery (Anti-Aircraft)
211th Coast Artillery (Anti-Aircraft)
213th Coast Artillery (Anti-Aircraft)
251st Coast Artillery (Anti-Aircraft)
260th Coast Artillery (Anti-Aircraft)
244th Coast Artillery 151mm Gun
250th Coast Artillery 151mm Gun
252nd Coast Artillery 151mm Gun
240th Coast Artillery (Harbor Defense)
241st Coast Artillery (Harbor Defense)
242nd Coast Artillery (Harbor Defense)
243rd Coast Artillery (Harbor Defense)
245th Coast Artillery (Harbor Defense)
246th Coast Artillery (Harbor Defense)
248th Coast Artillery (Harbor Defense)
249th Coast Artillery (Harbor Defense)
265th Coast Artillery (Harbor Defense)
105th Observation Squadron
119th Observation Squadron
154th Observation Squadron
116th Observation Squadron
MEMBERS
All members, both active and inactive, of
the units listed above.

President Franklin D. Roosevelt

CHAPTER 4

Heading West

*"The most persistent sound rever-
berating through the camp that
morning was the beating of war
drums in every Boy's heart."*

WITH THE DECLARATION of war from President
Roosevelt not yet 24 hours old, the Boys
were prepared to depart Camp Hulen. They
had no idea of where their final destination lay, only that they were heading west,
and probably into the Pacific Southwest
Theater of the war.

Earlier, when the command came down,
they were told to pack up and prepare the
trains for readiness. Having run this drill
a year earlier when they prepared to travel by train to Camp Hulen, they were in
a better position to respond. This time
they felt the sense of urgency in the air,
and saw a more serious look in the faces of their officers. They were to travel under blackout conditions, with coded

orders from Washington. At the time, the War Department wanted nothing to interfere with the Boys' arrival in Los Angeles. From there, they would board naval ships and be off to the Philippines and to the aid of General Douglas MacArthur. The Boys were given talks from senior officers on the importance of being ready "now that we are at war." Army Chaplains were also available for those who wished to talk. Excitement ran high as the Boys worked late into the night to ready the unit equipment for the trains and to pack up their own personal gear.

The Boys prepare to board the trains at Camp Hulen.

On Tuesday, December 9, reveille was sounded at 0530, one hour earlier than usual. Mess was quickly served, with the Boys required to use their mess kits, since all the unit crockery was packed up and already loaded on the train. Shortly after breakfast, the Boys were issued live ammunition and all weapons were checked. The unit was placed on standby alert with the order to be ready to board the trains at a moment's notice. Due to the "blackout" conditions, phones were off limits, which added to the anxiety that was already growing. The news of the attack on Pearl Harbor was on the front pages of every paper in the nation, the topic of every radio show and, thus, the concern of every loved one back home. Most of the Boys wanted to call home before heading out, but when they realized it was not possible, notepads and stationery appeared, with almost every soldier engrossed in getting his message on paper as quickly as he could, writing and readying for the camp postal clerk before the trains rolled. They all knew that once the trains started to roll, the opportunities to send mail would be few and far between.

The average age of the Boys was 21. Many hadn't traveled far from Massachusetts, and the trip to Texas was the furthest most had been from home. Now they were heading westward. Most were focused on thoughts of their families and girlfriends left behind, and all the memories they had accumulated in their young years. But not far from their main focus was the thought of the war that lay ahead. The most persistent sound reverberating through the camp that morning was the beating of war drums in every Boy's heart.

The Southwest Pacific Theater, where the Boys were heading, was a major theater of the war between the Allies and Japan. It included the Philippines, the Dutch East Indies, Borneo, Australia and its mandate Territory of New Guinea, and the western part of the Solomon Islands. This area was defined by the Allied powers' Southwest Pacific Area (SWPA) command. (8)

The Boys got the call to report to the trains at 1730. They were fed another meal at the depot, and then boarded their trains already loaded with guns, trucks and other equipment. By 2300 all were aboard and the Boys waited quietly for the movement they knew would eventually come. By 0015 Wednesday morning, they felt the rumble of the trains as they slowly started to move down the rails heading west.

The 211th was one of four Coastal Artillery units preparing to depart from Camp Hulen by train that morning. The other three, the

197th, 198th, and the 203rd, had all prepared in a similar manner as the Boys, and
were heading down the same tracks.

The Boys knew they were heading to the
Pacific. They also knew that no one was
there to say goodbye as the trains departed.

Most of the Boys fell asleep quickly.
They were sprawled out in the old boxcars,
and with their recently filled bellies,
along with the stress and worry of the
last 24 hours on their minds, most were
happy to sleep on the floor or against the
walls of their car. The convoy of trains
had been quickly summoned from other
train stations for this massive movement
of troops.

Johnny DeMello remembers the Boys, *"being
packed into the cars shoulder to shoulder.
All the cars had rigid bench seats facing
one another, and they were all rock hard."*

The trains rocked to a halt at 0715 in
the small town of Rosenberg, Texas. The
Boys were ordered to grab their gear and
get off their train cars, only to re-board
others further ahead on the tracks. To the
Boys' delight, the new cars had been converted earlier to comfortable Pullman-type
cars. From the sound of all the hooting and
hollering from the Boys upon the discovery
of their new rolling quarters, you would
have thought it was Christmas.

Each sleeping unit consisted of three beds (two down one up). Coins were flipped or rank pulled for the upper bunk. Once occupied, the shades were drawn and lights were dimmed low. There was just the hum of the speeding train and the occasional rattle of the tracks below them. The Boys knew what it meant. They were on their way to war.

The trains continued on for another ninety minutes or so before arriving in Temple, Texas. The boys weren't allowed to get off the train this time, but some of the "non-coms" were allowed to disembark and go into town to shop for supplies for the men.

Requests were placed for newspapers, magazines, playing cards, snacks, gum, cigarettes, stationary and anything else they could find in the short layover in Temple. Within less than an hour, the train was moving again. With new things to read and games to play, the Boys settled into their comfortable "home away from home on wheels."

The boys were then told that smoking onboard wasn't allowed and anyone caught would be assigned KP duty. A few cigarettes were quickly snuffed out.

During the next four days, their travel took them through the towns of Brownwood and Muleshoe, Texas, as well as Clovis, Vaughn, and Belen, New Mexico. At all the stops, the Boys were allowed to get off the trains and stretch their legs by doing calisthenics and exercises. A small unit of the boys was allowed to parade through the towns in formation. The spirit of the locals was apparent as many of the townsfolk showed their support by flying the flag and cheering on the Boys. It was not uncommon to see someone from the crowd reach out and hand the soldiers homemade baked items and other goodies. Obviously, the word was out that the Boys were heading west and off to war.

While they were heading west, other train convoys were also moving across the country carrying additional Army, Navy and Marine personnel, and vital military armament.

On December 11, somewhere between Top Rock and Welch County, Arizona, in a remote part of the country, one of the trains carrying the 211th *"lurched drunkenly, careened off the track, and crunched into the cinder-banked roadbed."* (Wyman Riley/Sunday Notebook/Vallejo TH) The Boys were jostled by the sudden and startling stop. They sat still for a moment, unsure what was happening, but word soon spread that the train had derailed. At least that was the official word being handed down through the ranks. For years to follow, it was suspected that some form of sabotage had occurred. With all the heavy train movement at that time, the likelihood of such a sabotaged event was unlikely, and the derailment was probably due to the heavy usage of the rails. Sabotage was never proven and became a story often repeated at the future reunions the Boys would hold.

This unexplained derailing, however, did change the course of the train and that of the 211th's fate. The train would be delayed for 24 hours, and the continued movement of the remaining trains was crucial, thus, causing the Defense Department to draw up new orders. With the coming of daybreak, the new orders had arrived. All the trains except those of the 211th were to continue onward to Southern California, while Colonel Hall's trains, once repaired, were to head north to a destination somewhere in the northwest.

The rolling wheels of these trains represented the first wave of the mighty U.S. rail transportation industry's role in assisting the U.S. war effort. When President Roosevelt delivered his "Arsenal of Democracy" speech to the nation in 1940, the train industry had already begun its part of moving needed military supplies across the country, which in turn, would eventually aid the country in recovering from the Depression.

The World War II years of 1941 to 1945 are considered by many historians to be a high point in the railroads' contribution to this country. The battles in Africa, Europe and the Pacific would have to be won, but this could not happen unless there was victory on "the Home Front." This was a war of movement that the USA had to win. (9)

What the Boys of the 211th learned years later was that many of the soldiers on the other trains in their convoy would eventually reach their final destination, the Philippines. From there they were transported onward into the Battle of Bataan. Many never returned home.

The Boys' new destination was to a place called Mare Island. As the word spread among the Boys, many assumed that they were still heading north and then out to some far away island in the Pacific. Little did they know as they continued to travel by rail through the cities of Needles, Bakersfield, Stockton and Sacramento, California, that their final destination would bring them into the San Francisco Bay Area community of Vallejo, California, home of Mare Island Naval Shipyard.

CHAPTER 5

Somewhere on the West Coast

"San Francisco Bay was more than just an arsenal and a production cornucopia. For 1,650,000 men, it was the last part of the States that they glimpsed before they saw combat, and it was the first thing that they saw when they returned." (10)

GOLD WAS DISCOVERED in California in 1849 and the great stampede from the east coast was underway. The sudden migration westward made it imperative for the United States to establish a naval base on the west coast from which ships of the Pacific Squadron could operate, and, as needed, be repaired.

In 1850, Commodore John Drake Sloat was ordered to lead a survey party in quest of a logical location for the nation's first naval installation on the west coast. Sloat, who had claimed California for the United States four years earlier at Monterey, recommended the island across the Napa River adjacent to the small settlement of Vallejo.

In 1852, the 800 acres was purchased by the United States.

Early Spanish explorers had called this long, low island "Isla Plana," or flat island. Legend has it that the name was changed when an old white mare owned by General Mariano Guadalupe Vallejo, Mexican commandante for Northern California, fell off a raft while being ferried across Carquinez Strait and swam ashore on the island. Vallejo renamed it "Isla de la Yegua," or Mare Island.

In 1853, Secretary of the Navy James Dobbin chose Commander David G. Farragut to take the task of converting the land claimed by Sloat into Mare Island Naval Shipyard. Farragut would take command of the island in 1854.

During the course of the next 90 years, prior to the attack on Pearl Harbor, Mare Island built and dispatched ships of all types. From the first wooden steamer *Saginaw* in 1859 to the submarine *Trigger SS237* in 1941, the inventory included over 100 ships, including submarines, destroyers, heavy cruisers, gun boats, sub chasers, ferries, tugs, barges and a battleship.

The City of Vallejo was named after General Vallejo, a military commander, politician and rancher. But many consider the real founder of the city to be John B. Frisbie. Upon Frisbie's marriage to Vallejo's daughter, Epifania, he was granted complete control of the land and its usage.

Frisbie worked tirelessly to establish the legitimacy of his father-in-law's land. General Vallejo deeded the city to Frisbie in December 1854 for $25,000, and Frisbie, in turn, employed E.H.Rowe to lay out the streets in the city. Most of the street names came from Rowe's design. During this period, Frisbie learned that the United States was investigating sites for a Pacific Coast naval base, and heard that a commission was considering building a shipyard in nearby Sausalito. Frisbie became proactive in lobbying for a new commission, and afterwards convinced the Federal government to change its recommendation to Mare Island.

Thus, a marriage of the two, the naval shipyard and the city of Vallejo, was inevitable. For the next 150 years, the two partnered and grew, relying on the resources that both had to offer.

By 1888, Vallejo had become a viable community and was starting to experience a population boom. As the Navy's needs increased, so did the production requirement of the shipyard. This increase meant more civilian employees, which led to more homes, retail shops and other services within the community. As the cash started to flow from hand to hand, nicer homes could be seen being built on the hills of Vallejo. Larger commercial and government buildings replaced earlier structures.

By the mid-1930s the city's population was close to 30,000. Although other communities throughout the United States were still reeling from the Great Depression, Vallejo was fast becoming a viable and rich community. Due to the increased work demands of the shipyard and the large federal payroll that soon followed, spending of that income would soon flow into the local businesses, both legal and not so legal, and Vallejo would eventually pick up the moniker of "City of Cash."

Roger Lotchin, professor of history at the University of North Carolina, stated, *"San Francisco Bay was more than just an arsenal and a production cornucopia. For 1,650,000 men, it was the last part of the States that they glimpsed before they saw combat, and it was the first thing that they saw when they returned."*

Thus, when the Japanese attacked Pearl Harbor on that infamous Sunday, it was an assumed fact that the west coast of California would be their next target.

CHAPTER 6

The Batteries

"A giant cannon aimed at the Pacific."

As the expression, *"A giant cannon aimed at the Pacific"(11) alluded to,* the 211th was just one small part of the larger plan to protect the Pacific Coast and its cities at the time. Coastal AA gun emplacements were placed up and down the entire west coast, with a high concentration being in the San Francisco Bay Area.

By 1940, Battery Townsley and Battery Davis were in place overlooking the Golden Gate, designed to protect the San Francisco Bay Area from enemy air and sea attack. The importance of the Bay Area from a military standpoint would be measured later, when the Bay Area would become responsible for almost 45 percent of all the cargo shipping tonnage and 20 percent of warship tonnage built in the entire country during World War II. (12)

Mare Island would lead the parade of ship builders that would go on to build "a ship a day." totaling 4,600 ships during the 1,365 days of war. Compared to the decade before 1940, when the entire country launched only 23 ships, the "ship a day" formula would go on to mark an astonishing time in American ship-building history. World War II shipbuilding would go down as perhaps the greatest combined effort of government and private industry in the nation's history. (13)

When the Japanese attacked Pearl Harbor, our military leaders knew the importance of the Bay Area's potential role in our west coast defense. The government quickly ordered all military personnel to return to their units and the west coast defenses were put on full alert.

The command center for all these recently deployed coastal fortifications was in an underground facility at Fort Winfield Scott, Presidio, San Francisco, and dubbed, *"Harbor Defense Command Post/Harbor Entrance Command Post"* (HDCP/HECP). (14)

The HDCP/HECP was a guarded operation, known only by senior military staff, and its role was crucial in the defense of the west coast. The command center coordinated all the batteries used to defend the Bay Area against enemy sea or air attack, and also tracked and coordinated all shipping traffic in and out of the Golden Gate.

When the train cars carrying the Boys finally arrived outside Vallejo, in American Canyon, they were met again with a downpour of rain as they rumbled to a stop. The Boys sank up to their knees in mud as they jumped from the cars, and the heavy equipment quickly sank to the axles as it was being unloaded. The Boys were quick to reference Patton's earlier observation and could be heard asking, *"Are we in hell yet?"* The 211th Coastal Artillery Regiment, First Corps of Cadets had finally arrived.

Corporal John DeMello was assigned to HQ as an administrative assistant, and, thus, quickly got assigned to naval housing near the officers upon his arrival. *"Most of the other men were sent out to the south end of Mare Island or various parts of Vallejo, and had to dig dugouts to sleep in. They were miserable. I felt bad for them. I also felt lucky,"* he said.

The Boys' primary mission was the protection of Mare Island, Vallejo, and the surrounding communities of Crockett, Richmond and Hamilton Field. Upon their arrival, they would tactically set up their own network of batteries consisting of their mobile anti-aircraft 90mm cannons, searchlights, observation posts and radar stations.

Each battery was designed to be a self-sufficient group of approximately 60 to 180 men who provided around-the-clock watch of their position. Most of the batteries were equipped with the 90mm cannons, which served as the Army's primary heavy anti-aircraft gun. The 90mm was the largest size weapon that could be manually loaded at high elevations, which served the 211th since most of their batteries were set up on hillsides around the town.

The Boys were also armed with .50 caliber machine guns, which fired lead and tracer ammunition. One reported location of one of the .50 caliber guns was on top of St. Vincent Ferrer high School because of the rooftop's high bird's-eye view of the city.

Wyman Riley, Editor of the Vallejo Times Herald, wrote in his Sunday Notebook in 1962,

"Out on Sears Point Road, about 200 yards west of Guadalcanal Village, Battery A was secreted in what looked like an honest-to-goodness motor court. Back then, they weren't called motels. The innocent- looking motor court, marked by its "No Vacancy"

sign and incongruously patrolled by armed guards, suddenly became a small deadly arsenal when its roof rolled back to disclose big anti-aircraft guns."

Riley would go on to describe the other battery locations: "Battery B was on the south end of the island on what is now the golf course. Battery C was east of Highway 40, where the Highway 80 currently runs and crosses Fleming Avenue and its guns were concealed beneath slide-back roofing designed to look like tennis courts."

Battery D was located in the hills of Crockett. Battery E was spread out with four guns located at the Kaiser Shipyards in Richmond. There were two guns looking over the Carquinez Bridge, one sitting in the Carquinez Highlands, and one on the bottom of Solano Avenue looking over the Vallejo waterfront."

Other locations were at the Federal Terrace Hill, Washington Park and the Vista Hill. Vallejoan Jim Walsh, who grew up in Bay Terrace on B Street, remembers, "Hearing the gunfire overhead, as the soldiers would shoot at targets on the west side of Mare Island. The targets were made up of canvas banners, pulled by our low-flying planes."

Somewhere on the West Coast

Also located throughout town were spot-lights and "listening devices," better known as sound locators, used to locate incoming enemy planes.

The 211th training to use Sound Locators.

The sound locators worked in conjunction with the spotlights and the anti-aircraft guns. It was during World War II that searchlights formed part of a system of aircraft detection linking locator devices, searchlights and anti-aircraft (AA) guns.

Searchlights

The locators sent electronic information to the lights and the guns, which in turn tracked the target in synch with each other. Once a locator locked on to an aerial target, the concept was for both lights and guns to be trained on the target, (via the height and distance data received from

the locator) so the target could be nearly simultaneously illuminated and then de-
stroyed. Locators were first based on sound
and heat detection, and, ultimately, radar
became the preferred method of target acquisition. Units were generally separate,
but advances in radar technology late in
the war saw the integration of radar into
both searchlight and AA gun designs. Anti-
aircraft artillery accuracy was at stake,
both from tactical and economic points of
view. In 1940 in England, for example, it
took an average of 20,000 rounds of ammunition to down a single enemy aircraft! The
demand for more accurate methods of engaging, tracking and destroying aircraft, especially at night, was driven by the need
to destroy more targets without expending
lots of ammunition. (15)

2nd Battalion Headquarters (HQ) for the
211th was set up in the Veteran's Hall building across from the city park. Here, Colonel
Hall received communications from the HDCP/
HECP on a daily basis, and, in turn, passed on
the information to his junior officers, who
would relay the information on to the Boys,
as needed. Several hundred soldiers were billeted in the building, in addition to those
pitching tents across the street in the park.

The headquarters was a hub of activities,
with information being transmitted to and

from all batteries in the area. Special attention was focused on Batteries A, D and E because of their strategic locations outside the city limits.

Battery A was out on Highway 37, Battery D in the hills of Crockett and Battery E near the Richmond shipyards. Colonel Hall's junior officers would also keep in constant contact with Battery C, monitoring and directing all the eastbound and westbound traffic on Highway 40 and keeping the Carquinez Bridge clear.

As the days and weeks progressed, the initial fear of imminent invasion finally settled into a long-term resolve to defend Mare Island, Vallejo and the surrounding areas. The Boys were located on virtually every hillside overlooking the city, positioned in their sandbagged dugouts and camouflaged batteries, looking for the approach of a Japanese plane that would never come.

CHAPTER 7

Barrage Balloons

"They're going to get away every now and then."

JIM DAVIS, FORMER VALLEJO FIRE CHIEF AND A 211TH AA MEMBER

WHEN THE UNITED States entered World War II, a sudden fear swept the city of Vallejo. This was compounded by the immediate appearance of barrage balloons and citywide blackouts, all of which left the citizens of Vallejo fearing the appearance of enemy aircraft.

The primary use of barrage balloons during World War II was to prevent attacks by low-flying aircraft. Heavy cables were used to tether gas-filled balloons, which hovered from a few hundred up to 4,000 feet high. Any dive-bombing aircraft had to avoid their cable tether, which could easily tear a wing off and cause the plane to crash. Besides negating low-level attacks, the balloons forced other planes to fly higher than intended on bombing runs, thus, affecting their accuracy. They also enhanced ground-based air defenses by giving the anti-aircraft artillery units easier visibility to their targets, since intruding aircrafts were limited in altitude and direction. Finally, the ground cable presented a definite mental hazard to pilots who had to focus on the cables while navigating towards their target.

The balloons could be raised or lowered to the desired altitude by a winch. Balloons varied in size but, on an average, were approximately 62 feet in length and 25 feet in diameter. (16)

The soldiers who made up the 309th Barrage Balloon Regiment arrived in Vallejo in June 1942, and began to set up their batteries throughout the city. The 309th came into town from Camp Tyson, Tennessee and, soon, a friendly rivalry developed between the 309th and the 211th. The original 211th Boys complained that the 309th was *just a bunch of draftees who were sloppily dressed and played with balloons.*

While in Vallejo, the 309th would use the facilities at Vallejo High School as their headquarters and also used the school grounds for repairs of balloons. The balloons needed to be hauled down regularly to be examined, and often repaired. Patching of the small holes that appeared in the balloon surface material was a common task. The anchoring cables also required frequent repair work. The routine established was to lower each balloon at a specific time during the day to its anchoring pad. Each anchoring pad consisted of eight to 10 soldiers, who checked for leaks and any other damage to the balloons and cables, and then return them to their raised position. The balloons in the Vallejo area were estimated to be about 2,000 feet in the air. The 211th assisted the barrage balloon units by providing around-the-clock security at the perimeter of each balloon site.

Precisely how many balloons comprised a battery was a military secret at the time, but Vallejoans could look skyward and see many of the monster-like balloons floating casually over the greater Vallejo area. The sight of the balloons did bring a grim realization to the citizens of the fact that America was at war and that Vallejo was part of this new combat zone.

Barrage balloon near downtown Vallejo waterfront.

Balloons could also be seen hovering over the north and south ends of Mare Island. Additional balloons reached as far east to the Suisun marshes, with one actually located on the Golden Gate Duck Club, south of Cordelia. Another was located near San Pablo Bay on the west, and another on the north end of Highway 37. In Vallejo, some of the locations cited by witnesses were in the Carquinez Heights area, Federal Terrace area, Washington Park, St. Vincent

Ferrer School, St. Vincent's Cemetery, Grant School, the Magazine Hill area, and the field by the intersection of Tuolumne Street and Solano Avenue.

The barrage balloons apparently provided the citizens of Vallejo more excitement than the enemy. The balloons were at high risk of breaking away from their stanchions, and became an even greater risk with high winds. Such was the case in the fall of 1942, when tornado-like winds hit Vallejo, coming in off San Pablo Bay. The winds were so strong, that a balloon tethered near the Federal Terrace housing area broke loose and hit a power line, causing the balloon to explode. The explosion took the life of one soldier, and injured 10 civilians. Over a dozen Federal Terrace homes were damaged. Newspapers reported that debris was scattered over a 200-yard area. Most of the families in the area had to be evacuated.

Linden Harpine, who served with the 309th while in Vallejo, recalled the impact of the hydrogen-filled balloon exploding on its pad in the Federal Terrace neighborhood, and how it inflicted several casualties at the time. *"It actually flattened some of the public housing units in its blast area."*

Vallejoan Don McDermitt recalled a barrage balloon unit situated west of the old cemetery on Sacramento Street. He and his buddies would often go after school to hang out with the soldiers. They especially looked forward to talking to the Boys because they liked their Bostonian accents. Sometimes they were even able to scrounge a little treat from the cook's tent.

Don also recalled hearing the explosions of several balloons and feeling the shock of one near his home. He recalls the high winds gusting through the area, followed by the explosion.

Another explosion occurred when a balloon anchored at Washington Park broke loose and drifted awhile until it snagged a power line near the 100 block of El Camino Real Avenue, causing power outages to the homes in the area.

Juanita Gass, a young girl at the time, remembers, *"One of the balloons coming down in an alley right behind our house in the 100 block of Kentucky Street. It hit a telephone pole wire and just exploded. It's a wonder no one was injured because there was a house right under the balloon. We knew everyone in the neighborhood, and fortunately no one was hurt."*

Betty Precour, a student at St. Vincent Ferrer High School at the time, remembers the balloon on top of the school. *"The Boys slept at the school in the basement area,* but were all over the building and campus grounds. The Boys were also on the school roof and church tower watching for enemy aircraft and manning 50 mm machine guns."

The Vallejo Times Herald reported in 1942, *"The uptown areas of Vallejo were without electric current for a short time, when an escaped barrage balloon hit a tension wire at Trinity and Ohio Streets, bursting into flames, burning the wiring, and causing a power failure."*

Shirley Coyne was seven at the time, but remembers clearly the barrage balloons in Vallejo. *"I was quite afraid of them. They looked very sinister to me. I also remember the blackout window shades everybody had. I remember the warning sirens that went off occasionally and the fear I felt at those times. And the worst thing of all for me, as a child, were those twisting, twirling searchlights in the sky at night! I was very, very afraid of them. And I continued to be afraid of them for several years after the war. I guess until I was about seven years old, I would never go outside at night if there was a searchlight in the sky. If for some unbeknownst reason I had to go out, I would run as fast as I could to get wherever I was going and I would never, ever look up! I didn't want to take a chance on seeing that moving searchlight.*

Or, worse yet, that searchlight finding me! Scared me to death!"

Vallejoan Charles Bailhache recalled a balloon located on the old AFL ballpark on Nebraska Street. It somehow lost a stabilizing fin and caught fire. *"This became a real challenge for the ground crew. What do you do with a burning balloon still at 1000 feet in the air? My parents called me inside once they found out the balloon was burning and going in circles at the end of the cables, much like a very slow rocket, and made a little hissing noise."*

Stephan White was a young boy attending Grant School at the time, and recalls, *"One corner of the playground occupied by a large barrage balloon installation. A small detachment of soldiers, who serviced the balloons and kept them flying, lived in the barracks across the street. Those soldiers, not much older than kids themselves, often played ball with us during recess and lunch."*

Stephan and his buddies returned to school one morning only to find the balloon and soldiers gone. *"Some of us seized the opportunity to check out the empty barracks, which contained remnants of their existence. There was a very large pile of books that had been left on the floor in the middle of the hut. We didn't wait for an invitation to help ourselves to the spoils of war."*

Criticism was rampant and directed at the use of the balloons by the Army. The neoprene-coated fabric was sometimes faulty and caused the hydrogen gas to lose purity due to entry of air. On occasion heat and sunlight caused decomposition of the neoprene, which resulted in the release of chlorine gas. This would combine with the hydrogen and water vapor produced by the hydrochloric acid, which then attacked and weakened the balloon fabric. Other problems included fabric tears, separation of seams due to poor cementing and winch malfunctions, all natural problems in the development of a relatively new technique. As Jim Davis, former Vallejo Fire Chief and a 211th AA member stated, *"They're going to get away every now and then."*

The balloons were probably considered by some to be the lesser of two evils, being that they were providing a deterrent to a possible air attack. The 309th was disbanded and pulled out of Vallejo on September 9, 1943.

Betty Tedesco, widow of 211th Bill 'Mosey' Tedesco, stated, *"The 309th was from the South, and just didn't quite have the polish and shine the 211th had. Colonel Hall was known as 'Spit Shine' Hall, and the 309th just didn't meet his standards. Rumor was, that when the 309th finally moved out of Vallejo, Colonel Hall ordered their camp-sites be burned, since he considered them a disgrace to the U.S. Army."*

CHAPTER 8

City of Vallejo During WWII

*"There is one front and one bat-
tle where everyone in the United
States — every man, woman, and
child - is in action, and will
be privileged to remain in action
throughout this war. That front is
right here at home, in our daily
lives, and in our daily tasks."*

PRESIDENT FRANKLIN D. ROOSEVELT

VIRTUALLY ALL OF Vallejo life was dictated by
the declaration of war on that infamous
day in December. That dictated life style
lasted until peace was declared four years
later.

With a quiet calm and a bit of cold an-
ger, the community would quickly start to
measure its needs to prepare for the war.
Vallejo was different than other cities in
the country at the time, regard to preparing for war. Vallejo not only would experience an incredible population growth

with the onset of World War II, primarily due to the influx of defense workers, but would also experience first-hand, the immediate deployment of military defenses from within its boundaries. The war movement was everywhere. The Boys would set up their anti-aircraft guns throughout the city, along with the spotlights and sound detectors. Later, those would be coupled with the barrage balloons batteries of the 309th.

The population would grow to over 90,000, almost three times the census count of 1940. Vallejo residents of all races and faiths, young and old, men and women, knew that working together to provide whatever aid was needed was an immediate requirement of all.

Finding housing for the large influx of workers coming into Vallejo would prove to be just one of many problems the city leaders would have to deal with. With the shipyard's employment growth, private construction couldn't keep pace with the ever-growing demand for housing.

The city, like others in the Bay Area, became a haven for assisted and shared housing. Families would rent out spare bedrooms, basements, attics and garages. Empty warehouses were converted to dorms, people would double up in single rooms, and everyone was willing to make a sacrifice.

Betty Tedesco, remembers, *"My parents buying a house at 233 Viewmont Street in 1941. My parents would add a room over the garage for my brother, and then, with my brother and me both away at college, they decided to fill our rooms with boarders."*

Betty also recalled when, *"My dad was driving around shortly after the Boys had arrived into Vallejo, when he saw these soldiers walking around in the rain in the Federal Terrace neighborhood. He came home and told my mother...they're kids, they're away from home, and it's Christmas. My mother wouldn't stand for it, so my dad went and picked them all up, and brought them back to the house. That's how we met the Boys. The Boys were quick to make our home a place to hang out. They liked to play cards a lot. My mom loved having them there and would always make homemade cakes for them. With all the roomers/boarders, and the Boys hanging out, the house was always crowded. My mom got thank you notes from the parents of the Boys for taking care of them. Bill would come over with the other soldiers, but he would always stand out from the others. This is where we first met. We were married the following October."*

———

Vallejo Mayor John Stewart would issue a proclamation calling together all members of the Civilian Defense Council to initiate an emergency city-wide plan. Sheriff Jack Thornton would direct all deputies to establish a twenty-four hour guard over the city waterworks and other vital areas. The California Highway Patrol would set up a watch at both approaches to the Carquinez Bridge, while the Coast Guard would patrol the straight.

An announcement came from Mare Island Naval Shipyard that the Yard was fully prepared to maintain the security of the base. Full wartime precautions would be put into effect and all sailors and Marines were ordered to return to their ships immediately.

Vallejoan Joanne Shiveley was nine years old at the time and remembers going into the city with her family, which included her brother-in-law, who was a career Marine. *"My family worked on Mare Island and we were getting ready to go into San Francisco at the time to visit friends of my parents. The news started to come in via radio and newspaper, as we arrived into the city. We might have been in the city for maybe just an hour when my brother in-law started to get antsy and said he had to get back to the base. By the time we got back to Vallejo, everything had been locked down and secured on Mare Island."*

Soon after the recall of all personnel, orders were issued to the Navy sentries to "shoot to kill," as precautions were tightened against possible sabotage at Mare Island Naval Shipyard. The order applied particularly to regulations providing "that lights of automobiles approaching sentries at night be extinguished" so sentries would not be blinded.

Air raid sirens were quickly installed near City Hall, Vallejo High School, and Grant School. Per Mayor Stewart, *"Should it become necessary to sound an air raid warning device during the day, all three would blast simultaneously."* The siren blasts were colored coded with yellow indicating an alert (a 3—5 minute steady continuous siren tone), and red indicating imminent attack (a 3—5 minute wail siren tone, or series of short tone bursts on devices incapable of wavering, such as whistles.)

Ex-Vallejoan Stephen White recalls being a student at Grant School when the sirens went off. *"We would hide under our desks as practiced many times before. We knew it was just a drill but hoped that something exciting might happen. Of course, it never did."*

Blackout curfews were also established. Blackout wardens would patrol neighborhoods at night, knocking on doors to admonish residents who had left a light burning after the familiar air raid siren had wailed. Vallejoan Don McDermitt remembers being a young boy at the time and recalls, *"All the neighbors putting up blackout curtains on their windows."*

As the days and weeks progressed, the initial fear of imminent invasion settled into a long-term commitment to defend the city by every means possible. Vallejoans would scan the skies for the inevitable air attack, which fortunately never came.

The Vallejo Times Herald reported in 1942.

Vallejo has gone a long way in civilian defense work since that first blackout, a day after the Pearl Harbor attack. It was a panicky town when the lights dimmed that evening of the eighth, and hundreds of civilians milled around the police department and the city hall. On their lips was the question, "What can I do?"

The Civilian Defense Council, headed by Mayor John Stewart, and his able assistants, following the state mandate, soon told them what they could do. Disaster and medical groups were formed using civilians, police officers and firemen.

"*We have improved more than it is pos-sible to estimate. We shudder to think what could have happened had we been attacked the day after Pearl Harbor. Our efficiency then was nothing. Now it is a different story. We have improved more than 200% at least, since that time.*"

Vallejo would hold various drills through-out the city after the attack on Pearl Harbor, in preparation for further attacks by the Japanese. Some of the drill in-volved newly formed medical teams who would man the first aid stations.

The City had 12 major first aid sta-tions, and 65 secondary stations. Six of the major stations were designated "ca-sualty or injury stations," where doctors and nurses would be available if any at-tacks occurred.

Vallejoan Margaret Anthony recalled her parent's home at 1776 Broadway Street be-ing used as one of the small hospitals. The Garibaldi Hospital Unit, # 5, as it was referred to, was one of the 12 residences chosen to be a major first aid station. Elsa Widemann, who at the time was head of the local Red Cross, approached Margaret's parents to use their basement playroom as a hospital. The feeling back then was that if the Japanese did attack the west coast, there would be a greater need for hospital beds than what currently existed. Margaret recalled hospital beds with white linens being set up, along with a small treatment room.

The residential hospitals were staffed with a registered nurse who oversaw the volunteer staff that was made up of neighbors from the community. The nurses would teach the residents first aid skills required to respond to a disaster.

Residential hospitals were also set up in the First Methodist Church at 502 Virginia Street and the First Baptist Church at 2025 Sonoma Boulevard. The City of Vallejo would also contract with Napa State Hospital to have them make 200 medical beds available, if needed. Fundraisers were common and would be organized by the nurses to raise funds to buy first aid supplies for their individual units.

All of the warring nations relied on propaganda, the spreading of selective facts and loaded messages, to promote a cause. The U.S. was no exception. Federal agencies like the Office of War Information (OWI) found that the simple poster was a cheap, flexible, and effective propaganda tool.

During this period of time, both of the local newspapers, the Times Herald and the Evening News Chronicle, were keeping their readers abreast of the conditions at home and abroad by including coverage of the war through stories, pictures and updated reports on progress. Caricatures of Hitler, Hirohito, and other war figures appeared frequently.

War posters could be seen everywhere throughout the city of Vallejo. Post office walls, city hall, sides of buildings, hotel lobbies, libraries, stores, restaurants and schools all had the propaganda in clear view.

Every man, woman, and child would be reached and moved by the message. Thanks to the posters, the distant war was a vivid presence in the lives of all.

Using bold colors, dramatic images, and concise wording, war posters and magazine covers made it clear who the country's enemies were, reminding Americans of the sacrifices made by enlisted men and women overseas. They also detailed the numerous ways average citizens could contribute to the war effort. As one popular poster put it, "We can, We will, We must!"

This would only add to the already profound sense of patriotism that was growing within the community. This really came into effect when the government announced the need for rationing. Vallejoans were encouraged to save grease, tin, metals, paper and, especially, rubber.

The Japanese had seized plantations in the Dutch East Indies that produced 90% of America's raw rubber. President Roosevelt called on citizens to help by contributing scrap rubber to be recycled. Gas stations in Vallejo would become collection centers for used tires and other rubber items.

Voluntary gas rationing would prove ineffective, and by the spring of 1942, mandatory rationing was needed. Rationing of gas would become part of everyday life in Vallejo after it was implemented. It was initiated not so much to save fuel, as to save tires and the rubber of which they were made. A nation-wide speed limit of 35 miles per hour was also enforced to save the wear and tear on tires.

To ration gas, the government issued coupon stamps. These "A" stamps were worth three to five gallons of gasoline per week for essential activities such as shopping, attending church, and going to the doctor. The letter on the stamp would have matched a sticker on the car's windshield. People using their cars for work could buy more gasoline, and truckers could buy all they needed.

Per the Vallejo Times Herald, the Vallejo Rationing Board issued the following explanation of the value of gasoline ration coupons after considerable discussion with Vallejo motorists:

1. All passenger cars~Class A - 4 gallons
2. Service vehicles~Class T-1 - 5 gallons
3. Non-Highway~Class E - 1 gallon
4. Official and fleet~Class B - 4 gallons
5. Motorcycles~Class D - 1 1/2 gallons

Prior to the rationing imposed by the city, gasoline sales hit an unparalleled high as citizens jittery over prospective rationing staged a "run on the tanks." Motorists besieged service stations in all parts of the city, spurred by the false rumor that all gasoline sales would be frozen in preparation of the upcoming rationing.

Other items rationed were sugar, coffee, meat, dairy products, fats and oils. Vallejoans were asked to use all of the items on the list sparingly and to recycle when asked.

Recycling of fats and oils was needed to help produce glycerin, which was a vital ingredient for explosives. The American Fat Salvage Committee was created to urge housewives to save all excess fat rendered from cooking and donate it to the Army to produce explosives. One pound of fat supposedly contained enough glycerin to make about a pound of explosives.

In 1942, United States Manpower Chief Paul V. McNutt, under the review of President Roosevelt, predicted that the 1943 draft would call for every fifth man in civilian work to be assigned to either armed forces or vital industries. He unfolded a solution to the potential manpower problem - a sweeping five-point program to apportion the nation's human resources among the armed forces and essential industries. His plan would essentially create a "national pool from which needs of armed forces, agriculture, industry and essential civilian activities will be supplied."

His new five-point program read...

1. Allocation of manpower to the armed forces, war industries, agriculture and other essential civilian activities.

2. Efficient use of labor for war industries.

3. Mobilization of the nation's labor reserves.

4. Transfer of workers from less essential activities to activities essential to the support of the war.

5. Provision of labor needed for essential agriculture.

McNutt stated that the tempo of inductions into the armed forces would increase in 1943 until one out of every five men in the civilian labor force would be called up. The present ratio was one out of nine. Women would be required to fill 30% of the civilian work force.

One of those women coming to Vallejo for wartime employment was Dorothy Matrisciano, later known a Dot Mann. As an 18 year old, she and her sister-in-law came from Nebraska.

"I worked the swing shift at Mare Island and when work ended, I would go home, let my hair down (she had to keep her hair covered while on the job), put on a dress and go off to the swing dances at Farragut School. I enjoyed going to one of the many movie houses available at the time. The ValMar movie house advertised late shows for the convenience of the Vallejo defense workers. It was a wild and crazy time back then. There was a lot of hustle and bustle. People were living for the moment. There

was never any complaining and a lot of sharing. Everything from gasoline, to coffee, to sugar, to shoes was rationed. I had trouble getting shoes. Leather ones were almost impossible to get."

Mann would eat most of her meals in the shipyard cafeteria, which at its height, was putting out almost 55,000 meals a day. *"I used to send my sugar stamps home. There were still five kids at home."*

CHAPTER 9

The Ranches

"When the Boys arrived on that rainy morning of Deccember 14, places in which to unpack, settle and dry out were few and far between."

DAVE LAWSON LIVED on the family ranch owned by his father-in-law, Frank Lewis. The Lewis Ranch was approximately 70 acres, consisting of two parcels of land in North Vallejo, and was divided by Highway 40, which ran through the middle of the ranch. The ranch, which was mostly farmland, had an abundance of fruit orchards throughout.

Upon the arrival of the 211th into the city, Dave, realizing that there was a shortage of housing for the 1,800 men, offered up his garage and a smaller outbuilding as a place for some the Boys to take shelter. The garage and coop were small, but offered an instant roof under which the Boys could sleep. Battery C, better known as the 211th motor pool, when offered the opportunity, took up residence in the two buildings, and over time added two additional buildings, which would eventually become their permanent barracks.

There was a very large grouping of eucalyptus trees on the ranch adjacent to what is now Hanns Park, thus, providing needed coverage for additional Army armament.

The Boys driving the dirt road near the Lewis Ranch.

A dirt road, which would later become Fairgrounds Drive, ran north and south and connected the Lewis Ranch to the north with the Minahan Ranch to the south. This became a well-traveled road for the Boys, especially Battery C.

Battery C was a very active bunch. One of its members, Bob Kukuruza, from Brockton, Massachusetts, was assigned to the motor pools operation because of his civilian experience in driving the larger trucks. Soon after arriving in Vallejo, Bob was put in charge of all the rolling stock and the important task of keeping Highway 40 open, since the movement of troops and supplies to and from San Francisco was vital. Bob and his crew were quick to respond if there was ever an accident or breakdown on the city streets or on the highway.

Bob and his crew were also known to discretely gather supplies from various parts of the city to help build some of the needed 211th structures. One story shared was how they would follow the Navy Seabees around from project to project during the day, taking inventory of their building supplies, and return at night to 'acquisition' their needed materials. Bob's crew became known as 'Bob's Midnight Raiders' for their stealth acquisitions.

Later in 1945, upon returning to Vallejo after the war, Bob would purchase a truck from the Army surplus, and open his own business, Bob's Tow Service.

Betty Tedesco shared the story, *"I was pregnant and driving downtown with my mother when we had a flat tire. I had the number to the motor pool and called Bill to come down and help. Well, my Bill arrived with Bob, but Bill, being the Italian he was, was very angry and probably a little embarrassed to have been called by me. But Bob said, 'Now Mosey, quiet down, we're just going to help Betsy Boo.' Years later, when Bob became ill, Bill would go and visit him about once a month. Bob would ask Bill to drive him around to all the various battery locations throughout the city, just to reminisce about the old days. I loved Bob. During the last year of his life, I would send him two bins of homemade cookies, one for him to take home, and one for his crew."*

Another member of the 211th motor pool was Bill Pendergast. Bill was from Waltham, Massachusetts, and also had civilian experience driving heavy trucks. Bill would share the story of when he was asked to transport a nine-ton truck from Napa Junction to Mare Island shortly after the 211th arrival into Vallejo. At the intersection of Broadway and Tennessee Streets, a Marine MP directing traffic yelled for him to make a sudden right turn onto Tennessee Street. Bill later stated, *"I'm driving this nine-ton truck that's towing an eight-ton cannon with over*

200 rounds of high explosive ammunition, when the MP suddenly yells to turn right. It just so happens that there was a Texaco gas station on the corner. When I finally completed the turn and looked back, I noticed that the gas pumps were gone."

Bill was later deployed to Europe, but upon the war's end, returned to Vallejo and wed Daniel Lawson's daughter, Dorothy. Dorothy later told the story of how she first met Bill. *"I was standing on the corner near St. Vincent's, actually on my way home from school, when Bill pulled up in his Army truck. I guessed he recognized me from the ranch and offered me ride home. I didn't know who he was, but back in those days, you trusted everyone. Besides, he was a cute guy in uniform."* They eventually raised five children while Bill became one of Vallejo's prominent service station and auto repair business owners.

———

When the Boys arrived on that rainy morning of December 14, places in which to unpack, settle and dry out were sparse. Some lucky ones were given shared billeting in Navy and Marine barracks, but most of the Boys were expected to dig into the countryside while setting up their batteries.

Mrs. Nellie Minahan was another of the homeowners to reach out to the Boys. Her property, which consisted of approximately 30 acres, also sat on both sides of Highway 40. Nellie and her husband, Daniel, raised eight children on the property. Daniel, who was the Superintendent of Streets and Public Works for Vallejo in 1890, passed away in 1936. Nellie continued to live in the home with her four single daughters, Eileen, Alice, Lucile and Madeline. As soon as she heard of the Boys' need for shelter, Nellie opened her doors to the young men from Boston.

Mrs. Minahan and her four daughters adopted the entire Battery C, which was billeted just north of their property on the Lewis (Luis)* Ranch. Lonely, cold and wet, the servicemen could walk into the Minahan home and help themselves to a hot shower at any time of day or night. Shortly after their arrival, Nellie provided the resources for a new chapel and recreation hall, a 30 x 60 foot wooden structure painted white with a bell in the small tower that was constructed by the Boys in their spare time. The Boys followed the same plans used for Army camp halls throughout the US in designing and building this new structure. *(22)

Minahan Chapel

Upon completion of the new chapel, the city of Vallejo, in dedicating the beautiful new building, held a celebration. With city officials in attendance, Colonel Stuart Hall led the ceremony with the naming of Minahan Hall in Mrs. Minahan's honor as a token of appreciation for the Boys' regard for her kindness and hospitality to Army personnel. Mrs. Minahan also received the Regimental Insignia pin from Colonel Hall.

Mrs. Minahan receiving the Regimental Pin.

In their tribute, the men stated, *"Tracing our battery's history to the time we came here in the midst of "liquid sunshine," we came to know Mrs. Minahan during a time when we were pretty crudely set up with very few comforts, and because of her kindness, came to know her as Mom Minahan."*

"At that time, a shave or wash with hot water was almost unheard of, and through her kindness, we were allowed the use of her facilities in her own home. She gave

us a decent place to wash, words of kind-ness and a warm smile. She opened her house for all of us, offering a source of mental relaxation that bolstered the spirits of the men, whose morale, because of the bad weather and poor facilities, was at an ex-tremely low point. It was raining cats and dogs, and the only clean things we could bring to her parties were our hands and faces. We felt awkward in our dirty clothes and mud-soaked shoes, but this wonderful woman made us feel at home."

"About a month ago, we started work on this rather crude, rustic building of hers, and as it progressed, we became convinced that there was only one thing we could name it, and we all unanimously agreed to call it Minahan Hall."

The United Service Organizations for National Defense, USO, was brought into existence through presidential order on February 4, 1941 and was just coming into play in Vallejo during this time. Mrs. Minahan led the trend by holding her own socials in her home and newly built rec-reation hall. She and her four daughters, along with many other young women from the Catholic community, entertained the Boys by providing dance partners to the in-house music provided by the Boys themselves. It wasn't uncommon for a song to break out, and one often heard was the Irish ballad "Danny Boy," a favorite of the Boys.

The surviving widows of the Boys later told the same story of how they were warned by their parents to stay clear of those soldiers from the East Coast. The local young women of Vallejo were enamored by the Boys. They loved their pressed green uniforms with the brass buttons framing their Bostonian accents.

Romances were inevitable and Mrs. Minahan often served as Cupid with marriages soon following. The first wedding held in Minahan Hall was in December 1942, solemnizing the marriage of Miss Thelma Marie Showalter of South Dakota and Sergeant Morman W. Lasswell.

Another marriage in the Hall was between a young soldier, a Jewish man, who tried to make arrangements to marry his sweetheart in his hometown of Boston, only to have his request for leave denied. Upon hearing of the young man's concerns, Nellie stepped forward and made arrangements to have the wedding held in her hall, and for his fiancée to travel to California. She reached out to the community and found a rabbi. The young man's entire battery was invited, and for those who were able to attend, Nellie provided the traditional yarmulke caps.

Years later, Minahan Hall would become what is known as the American Legion Post. It was later replaced by the current building on Admiral Callaghan Way.

Author's note: My father, Leo, met my mother, Elaine Tracy, at one of Mrs. Minahan's socials, while he was playing his fiddle in a sing-a-long with the gals and guys at the get-together. My mom was serving as a hostess for the Catholic Daughters' Association. They were married in October 1942.

CHAPTER 10

The Band

"I carried my trumpet and mouth-
piece with me the whole time
I was in Europe, including the
Battle of the Bulge, I don't know
why. Many, many times I would
say, 'God, if you would only take
me back to Vallejo.'"

AL ROBINSON

THE BAND'S OFFICIAL title was the *211th Coastal Artillery Anti-Aircraft Regimental Band.* When the band members, approximately 100 of them, were ordered to load the trains back at Camp Hulen in preparation to go west, they would assist in getting the trains readied, but were more focused on their own specialty equipment that only they were trained to use. Their musical instruments, the drum-sets, brass instruments, reeds and strings were packed up along with the armament and ammunition. While at Camp Hulen, the musicians, in addition to drilling with their military colleagues, were "all ears" with the fine-tuning of their musical skills; the skills that they knew would come into play once they went off to war. These instruments were their weapons of choice, and they would practice often, fine-tuning those skills.

Marching Drill at Camp Hulen

Music was always a big part of the 211th. From their onset in Boston, during their training in Texas and Louisiana and their trip westward, the 211th had an incredible group of talented musicians who accompanied them. Bostonians Robert Carnes, Joe Toronto, George Cristo, Ralph Creeden and Webster Inglis joined Al Robinson and

Edward "Red" Graham in leading the group westward on their trip to Vallejo.

Home For the Aged

The band would be entering into the Vallejo community, a community that was predominantly made up of Navy and Marine personnel, and they would bring a sound unlike anything previously heard to the musical scene in the city.

As officer in charge of the 211th, Colonel Hall, a big music buff, went out of his way to recruit musicians for the unit. His first big move was to arrange for the nucleus of Bob Crosby's swing band - saxophonist Gil Rodin, jazz drummer Ray Bauduc and keyboardist Ray Sherman, to be transferred to the 211th. Colonel Hall's goal: to help keep the city of Vallejo entertained and to enhance the future sales of war bonds.

Before joining the 211th, Gil Rodin played saxophone, clarinet, flute and trumpet for Bob Crosby, prior to moving to California where he played with Harry Bastin. Rodin also did studio work and played with Red Nichols' radio band. He made his only recordings as a leader in 1930-31, amounting to four tracks, which included Jack Teagarden on vocals, as well as Eddie Miller and Benny Goodman as sidemen. (23)

Gil Rodin (right) with Lt. Farnum

Later in his career, Rodin did work in radio and television production, with Bill Cosby, among others. He produced the soundtracks to the films "American Graffiti" and "The Sting."

Ray Bauduc was a jazz drummer best known for his work with the *Bob Crosby Orchestra* and their band-within-a-band, *The Bobcats*. His New Orleans origins instilled in him a love for two-beat drumming, which he retained even when he played with Crosby. His stint with the *Bob Crosby Orchestra* would bring him national fame when he co-composed, with bassist Bob Haggart, two of the bigger hits that the *Bob Crosby Orchestra* would record, "South Rampart Street Parade" and "Big Noise from Winnetka."

Ray Bauduc on the drums at a
Mare Island bond drive.

His style, making use of woodblocks, cow-bells, the China cymbal and tom-toms, made him stand out from most drummers of the swing era. (24)

Ray Sherman appeared as a pianist on the Tommy Dorsey "Amateur Swing Contest" radio program from the Chicago Theater, winning first prize on the West Coast repeat broadcast. After being discharged in 1946 from the Army, his career took off and rewarded him with work in the radio and television industry. His radio career included shows with Abe Burrows, Judy Canova and Phil Harris.

For a while, Ray appeared as pianist and conductor on Bob Crosby's daily live TV show. From the late 1950's to the late 1970's, Ray devoted his time almost exclusively to free-lance work on records, motion picture sound tracks and television, both live and taped. Some of the big names with whom he worked were Henry Mancini, Nelson Riddle, Billy May, Frank Comstock and Johnny Green. Ray also did work the films "West Side Story," "Lil Abner," "Bye, Bye Birdie," and "The Days of Wine and Roses." His television work included "The Hollywood Palace,"" Adam 12," "Emergency," "Route 66" and "Happy Days."

Pianist Ray Sherman

Colonel Hall wasn't finished with trying to bring the best band possible to Vallejo. He was also successful in getting Vallejo native Joseph Graves, a trumpet player, transferred from 515th Engineer Battalion in Shreveport, Louisiana into the 211th.

Joe was the younger brother of Barney Graves, who himself was a well-known musician in the Vallejo area. Prior to the war, Barney had put together a 4-piece combo called the *Four Aces*, which included his brother, Joe. Barney would serve in the Army Air Corp, but would return to the area after the war to continue his musical endeavors up till the 1970's.

4 Aces with Joe Graves on the trumpet

Brother Joe would later go on to perform worldwide with some of the best big bands in the country, and at one point, took over for Harry James as the leading trumpeter for his band, *His Music Makers*, when Harry had to leave the band to go serve his country. (25)

Dixie Group with Joe Graves, Ray
Bauduc & Dink Thompson

Another group of musicians that Colonel
Hall sought out were the *Hobergs Among the
Pines* band, recruited in their entirety
with the promise that band members would
not have to serve overseas, but would remain stateside during the war. The members
of the Hobergs group were Rex Deal, Duane
Soares, Russ Mayes, Ken Eckland and 'Dink'
Thompson.

The 211th band would boast a marching,
a concert and a dance band. The sizes
of the individual bands usually ranged

from 15 to 30 musicians, depending on the Boys' availability, but together were over a 100 strong. Years later, many of the musicians felt that being deployed to Vallejo was probably the best musical gig at the time.

When the musicians first arrived in Vallejo on that cold and wet day, they assembled with their instruments and proudly paraded into the streets of the city creating quite a bit of excitement. Their presence may have helped calm the nerves of the local citizens by balancing the anxiety caused by the sight of the new anti- aircraft armament that also was rolling into the city.

Immediately after settling into temporary quarters at the Veteran's Hall on Alabama Street, band members were ordered by Colonel Hall to stow their instruments and to pick up their rifles. Colonel Hall ordered them to take on the full-time duty of becoming military police. Their battery's warrant officer, Earl Anderson, became the provost marshal for the group. Due to the large influx of 1,800 soldiers into the community, it became necessary to augment the Navy/Marine Police Battery, which at the time was made up of approximately 50 men.

The Boys were assigned to various key positions on the base, as well as important off-base sites throughout the city. Some of the off-base sites included a detachment of men out at the Blue Rock Springs area, with another at the Vallejo Yacht Club, where a guardhouse was set up out on a barge. Others would guard the Army motor pool on Mississippi Street. (26)

This assignment lasted about six weeks before the band was allowed to return to being full-time musicians. They needed a few days to rehearse to get back into shape, easing the task of becoming one of the best dance bands to which the city would get to "cut a rug."

Vallejoan Edie Baker remembers the band always practicing their parade formations on the street in front of the Portuguese Hall. The band was billeted in the basement of the hall at the time and it was not uncommon for the smell of cooking bacon to waft out to the public air as the kitchen crew cooked breakfast for the battery.

The band practicing in parade formation.

Before the war began, due to the challenges of the Depression and Prohibition, many of the local musicians struggled to make ends meet. Some survived by working during the day and playing at night.

With the ending of Prohibition, Vallejo began a transformation, which eventually gave it a reputation equal to that of San Francisco's Barbary Coast. This new influx of liquor-serving businesses created incredible opportunities for the local bands. From 1938 to 1939, the "Big Three" Vallejo night clubs, the Vallejo Country Club, El Nido and the Barrel Club, would all begin to provide "lavish" floor shows featuring out-of-town entertainers for their guests. (27)

Most of the cafes obtained liquor licenses, adding to the large number of bars serving liquor. Roadhouses converted to nightclubs, and in order to remain competitive, began to provide live music in their venues. Soon dance houses sprang up all around town. Other Vallejo venues included the Veteran's Memorial Center on Alabama Street and Rangers Hall.

With the onset of World War II, and the influx of 1,800 soldiers into the community, Vallejo recognized the need to provide for the recreational needs of the service personnel and defense workers assigned to the shipyard. They responded by building a new United Service Organizations (USO) facility at 225 Amador Street. The new facility debuted on January 28, 1942, just six weeks after the Boys' arrival.

For almost three years, Vallejo residents had a front-row seat to the 211th Band. The band, now with the addition of Rodin, Bauduc, Sherman and Graves, all wearing the Army green, was one of the first to perform at the new USO facility. The band would go on and perform locally at various other venues throughout the city, including the Veteran's Memorial Center, the YMCA and the Vallejo High School gymnasium.

The band's greatest contribution to the war effort was the selling of war bonds. These events were held up and down the California coast, backing such headliners as Bob Hope, Red Skelton, Jack Benny and the Andrew Sisters. They eventually helped raise over $7 million from the local community alone.

One such show billed as *"The Army Show,"* would be held twice during the spring of 1943, to sellout audiences. In order to purchase a ticket to the show, which later would be called *"one of the most outstanding shows ever presented in Vallejo,"* an individual needed to purchase a war bond first. The Boys practiced for the event right up until the night, keeping the acts a secret from the public. The show consisted of clever skits, solo numbers and big band and jazz ensembles.

A skit from the *"The Army Show"*

Another show was the *"Mare Island Follies*," that played in the summer of 1943 at Vallejo Junior High School. Billed as a 'fast moving' production of 17 scenes, featuring a mix of civilian and military acts, it was sponsored by Ship Building Contractors Barrett & Hilp, out of South San Francisco. A percentage of the sales also went to the Mare Island Hospital Brace Fund. At the time, Mare Island was considered one of the best in the manufacturing of prosthetic limbs, being dubbed the west coast amputation center for the wounded in the Pacific. (28)

Mare Island Follies

To cite an earlier Vallejo Times Herald article from June, 1943, *"Music by Benny Goodman or Bob Crosby couldn't cause more of a stir because the 211th Coastal Artillery Band is as jiving a gang as ever stirred the foot of a hep cat."*

The band also traveled into San Francisco to the studios of the Mark Hopkins Hotel, where they would hold recording sessions to cut 16-inch transcription records, which

were later heard by millions of troops overseas. These would later be transferred onto
12 inch "78" albums for public listening.

211th Regimental Band recording.

According to band member Al Robinson,
"We had pretty good chops in those days."
Robinson, a trumpet player, would later
gain fame in Vallejo with his own band,
The Robin-Aires. Robinson was later redeployed and ended up as a squad leader
with the 134th Infantry serving with General
George Patton. He was wounded at the Battle
of the Bulge in 1944. In an interview, he

recalled his three-month hospital stay as, *"The best part of my deployment because I didn't have to go back into combat again. I carried my trumpet and mouthpiece with me the whole time; I don't know why. Many, many times I would say, God, if you would only take me back to Vallejo." (29)*

CHAPTER 11

Redeployment

*"There was not a for-
mal agreement to return,
they just had the need to follow
their hearts."*

THE 211TH DILIGENTLY sat on alert at their watch stations, around the clock, for two and a half years, overseeing a vast network of coastal fortifications with anti-aircraft guns, sound stations, searchlights, observation posts and barrage balloons. By 1944, it was obvious to the Harbor Defense Command Post commanders that an invasion was a far-distant likelihood. The war was being fought overseas, in Europe and out in the Pacific. The Boys of the 211th were needed elsewhere.

The Boys were redeployed throughout the various campaigns in the world theaters, assigned to many different units. Battery E was redeployed within a month after its arrival in Vallejo, with most of the Boys assigned to anti-aircraft duty on ship convoys out in the Pacific.

Later, some went off to the 569th in the Asiatic-Pacific Campaign, while others ended up in the 126th Infantry Regiment serving in Europe, and were involved with the Omaha Beach campaign. Most of Battery A went north to the 419th Coast Artillery in the Aleutian Islands.

Some of the Boys went to Officer Training School, became officers, and were reassigned to combat units in the theaters of operation. Almost the entire regimental band was transferred to the 261st, and continued to support the war cause with their musical talents.

The last battery to leave Vallejo on December 12, 1944 was Battery G. They were redeployed for special maneuvers, and many were sent out as replacements in the various theaters of war.

Once the war ended, all the Boys returned home at various times, and to different separation centers throughout the United States to be discharged back into civilian life. The fact that so many of them returned to the Vallejo area speaks of the brotherhood that they carried with them while overseas. There was not a formal agreement to return, they just had the need to follow their hearts.

The Army weekly magazine "Yank," issue of September 29, 1944 wrote the following story about being separated, and what the Boys went through in a separation center near their homes during the last two days of their career in the US Army.

"When the Army decides that it no longer needs your services, you will be sent to a regional separation center in the United States. There, within 48 hours, you will be processed out of active service and either given a discharge or transferred into an inactive reserve unit.

The Army is establishing 18 of these separation centers in various camps all over the United States, with the intention of mustering out each GI at the center which happens to be the closest to his hometown.

You will spend your first day there getting your papers checked, listening to a few lectures on your return to civilian life and turning-in clothing and equipment. The Army takes back everything except one complete uniform, one extra shirt, gloves, ties, socks, underwear, towels, toilet articles, and personal belongings.

A physical exam takes up most of the second day. It is as complete as the exam you got at the induction station when you entered the Army. If there is something seriously wrong with your body or teeth that can be corrected, your discharge may be postponed until it is taken care of in a GI hospital.

After that, you sign your discharge papers and draw your money. You get all the pay due you, travel money, and $100 of your mustering-out pay. Mustering-out pay totals $100 if you've served fewer than 60 days in the States, $200 for more than 60 days in the states, and $300 if you have served any length of time overseas. The rest of your mustering-out pay is sent to you in $100 monthly installments after you leave the Army.

Then, with cash in your pocket, you get a free ride into town on a GI bus and a new start at home."

CHAPTER 12

The War Ends

From an article written by Jane Poole in the Vallejo Times Herald in the paper's August 15, 1945 edition.

JUBILATION RANG OUT over an anxiously waiting Vallejo yesterday as, at 4 p.m., the news of total victory and total peace swept the world. Screaming sirens and blasting horns heralded President Truman's declaration of peace, and throngs hysterical with joy paraded though the downtown streets.

The news came just as thousands of Mare Island workers were changing shifts, and the homecoming war workers joined with the crowds of shoppers and servicemen who seemed to literally pour into the Georgia-Marin area.

At the moment victory was officially announced, the City Hall siren started a blast that was joined by other local sirens, police equipment and private motorists' horns. The serpentine parade of cars with radios *and horns blasting continued through the city streets for many hours.*

The streets in the center of town were overrun by revelers, many who hailed passing motorists, and crowded on their running boards and fenders. Drivers who ventured into the Georgia-Marin district were met with a rain of confetti. Magazines and papers littered the streets.

Fender-scraping incidents were rampant as bystanders climbed over the passing cars and blinded the drivers with a storm of litter. No one seemed to pay much attention to the minor incidents in the general excitement that prevailed.

Sailors and youngsters, ransacking nearby alleys for inflammable material, started a huge bonfire in the middle of Marin Street, piling on boxes, crates and waste paper until the flames nearly touched telegraph lines.

Two Vallejo fire trucks quickly quenched the blaze and firemen discouraged further incidents by spraying overzealous leaders with hoses. Other minor fires kindled by the debris were quickly extinguished.

Major mischief of the celebration came when about 50 sailors lifted the bond booth at Georgia and Marin Streets from its base and deposited it in the center of the street. Broken glass from the building littered the streets with a passerby taking many of the record books to use as confetti.

Almost immediately after peace was announced, all local stores and bars closed their doors. A great number of eating-houses also shut their doors to celebrate the good news.

A liquor shortage was not noticeable in the streets of Vallejo in spite of the tavern shutdown. VJ Day bottles were much in evidence and sailors and girls shared them in impromptu toasts along the sidewalks.

Lipstick-smeared servicemen paraded the streets, singing at the top of their lungs and grabbing passing girls for victory kisses.

Exploding firecrackers and improvised bombs added to the earsplitting din of sirens, horns, overturned garbage cans and general uproar.

After sundown, the crowds thinned out considerably, but the thousands of Vallejoans who remained to welcome peace and victory in the street continued with full enthusiasm late into the night.

After the first early traffic jams, all midtown streets were closed into the night. The 300 block of Virginia Street was teeming with jitterbugging couples who danced to music broadcast from the Moose Hall dance. Other impromptu dances were happening throughout the city by celebrating groups.

As the victory revelry died down in the early morning hours and the shouting subsided, Vallejo was left with an overwhelming cleanup job. Remains of street fires, confetti, feather pillows and broken whiskey bottles covered the business district.

And as the first thrill of war's end passes, Vallejoans today will remember the boys who will not be coming back.

CHAPTER 13

The Brotherhood

"Marriages prospered and children would follow. Vallejo's birthrate started to shoot up as the Boys in uniform returned."

WHEN THE BOYS came together for the first time at Camp Edwards, they were strangers to each other. There were small pockets of boyhood friendships based mainly on affiliations with common neighborhoods. By the time the war had ended five years later, the Boys had become a very close-knit group. The bonds of war, faith, and the newfound love of Vallejo and the surrounding communities brought them closer than anyone would ever have predicted.

The Boys returned from various parts of the world. Years later, when asked why they returned to Vallejo, many stated the obvious: great weather and beautiful women.

John De Mello remembers visiting his parents in Massachusetts after returning from Europe. He was saddened by what he saw. His hometown still hadn't recovered from the Depression, jobs were scarce, and all around him he saw the results of industrial pollution. Add in the cold east coast weather and he was ready to return to Vallejo. It was upon his return to Vallejo that he met his future wife, Celeste.

There was no shortage of places to hang out upon their return. The two lower blocks of Georgia Street had a reputation of being a rough and reckless area and were said to have more nightclubs and bars per block than anywhere else in the world, including Singapore. The liquor was out front, gambling in the back and ladies upstairs. Often, the alleys behind the clubs had lines of GI's waiting to climb the stairs.

Active Navy and Marine personnel frequented most of the clubs and bars in the downtown area, thus, the Boys wanted a place to call their own. Being the gentlemen that they were, they wanted a place where they could bring their wives and girl friends without the threat of some drunken sailor wanting to intervene.

One of the first gatherings they had upon their return to Vallejo after the war was at the Channel Club on Georgia Street. The Boys had just returned to Vallejo and were eager to share their stories of war with their brothers.

Channel Club Ashtray

The Channel Club was located at 38 Georgia Street. It was owned and operated by Linc Raahauge, whose family also owned the Mare Island Ferry Company. Wanting their own place to hang out, the Boys approached Linc about renting out the top floor of his establishment and turning it into their own clubhouse. Linc agreed, a contract was drawn up, and the Boys sealed the deal by adding their own bar and building their own private entrance off the rear alley. The 211th Club had become a reality.

Officers were elected, club rules were written, stationery printed, a liquor license obtained and the bar stocked. Serving as the club president was Bill Pendergast, with Leo Cullen serving as vice president, Al McGinniss as treasurer, Bob Metcalf as recording secretary, and John DeMello as corresponding secretary.

211th Membership Card

Article XI of the Club's newly written constitution read: *"The object of this organization is to promote and maintain the spirit of comradeship, by social contact and mutual aid, that exists among former members of the 211th CA (AA) Regiment - First Corps of Cadets."*

Membership grew quickly as the Boys started to return to the city. The 211th Club would hold their first social function at the Vallejo Women's Club, an informal dance highlighted by a buffet supper and refreshments.

On another night, the Boys would hold a Cabaret Night at the clubhouse, with the entertainment provided by the Boys themselves. Some unforgettable moments were had. One act had some of the Boys dressing up as "can-can dancers," to the delight of the audience.

Cabaret Night 1947 ~ From L to R: James Lear, John Quinn, Tom Quinn, Joe Quinn, Fred Meggers, & Bill Pendergast

In keeping with the language of their Club Constitution, the Boys watched out for each other, just as they did during war times. One such occasion was when fellow 211th member Phil Bourgeois, a resident in Vallejo at the time, was involved in a serious automobile accident. The Boys gathered together to organize a fundraising event to help Phil with his living expenses. The benefit-dance would be called "Fun for Phil" and was held at the Casa de Vallejo Hotel. Local Vallejo musicians and professional entertainers from San Francisco teamed up to put on a fabulous floorshow in the hotel's Venetian Room, with headliner Helen Walker.

Unbeknownst to the Boys, they were fast becoming the parents of the generation later to be known as the "Baby Boomer" generation. Marriages prospered and children would follow. Vallejo's birthrate started to shoot up as the Boys in uniform returned.

211th Family Christmas Party ~ December 1947

In addition to the informal gatherings at the Clubhouse, the Boys organized reunions for the entire 211th Regiment every five years. The reunions were always well attended, with many of the Boys coming in from various parts of the country to attend. As the numbers grew, they were forced to hold their reunions in larger venues within the city.

The Boys held their last formal reunion in 1995 at the Vallejo Elks Lodge. The Boys referred to the reunion as the last "Big

One." Approximately seventy of the original 1800 211th Coastal Artillery Regiment attended from various parts of the country, with only ten still residing in the Vallejo area at the time.

211th 55th Reunion ~ 1995

Author's note: As of this writing in 2016, John De Mello is the lone Vallejo survivor of the original Boys from Boston.

CHAPTER 14

The Long and Short Tales of the 211th

The German Spy

VALLEJOAN BETTY PRECOUR shared the following story. Betty was a friend and classmate of Kate Hutchinson, whose mom was the proprietor of Mary's, the neighborhood grocery store located on the southwest corner of Florida and Santa Clara Streets, across the street from St. Vincent Ferrer High School. The school's location on the hilltop would become a vital point of interest for the Army. It placed a 50mm-caliber machine gun, along with spotters, on the roof of the school, and a barrage balloon was anchored nearby. It also served as billeting for a battery of soldiers. The soldiers could be seen coming and going at all hours of the day and evening.

Everyone who knew Mary Hutchinson knew she was a good citizen, but had no idea how important her role as storeowner would play in the war. Because store sat across the street from the school, it was always a hub of activity. She catered to the students during school hours and to the local families living in the neighborhood. Because of her store's location on the corner, Mary was able to witness, firsthand, the daily movement of the students coming and going, that of her neighbors, and now the Army, which had set up an encampment at the school.

Mary, in addition to running her store, also rented out the six small apartments above the store. Her typical tenants were the young men and women who had been hired to work at Mare Island. She felt it was her duty to accommodate these workers and, thus, didn't require deposits of any sort, offering renters credit in the store below.   One afternoon, a young man with a German accent applied for one of the vacancies. He appeared well dressed, well mannered, and came bearing cash to pay for three months in advance.   It was not until a few weeks had passed, that Mary noticed that her new tenant was spending most of his days and nights in his room. He would surface on occasion to buy groceries, always returning to his room. She also noticed that he never had visitors. This went on for several weeks, until she decided to share her observations with one of the officers of the 211th.

Her concerns were addressed later, when a group of government agents appeared with a warrant to search the apartment of her German tenant. Soon after, he was led away in handcuffs. It was revealed much later that Mary's tenant was a German spy assigned to watch the troop movement on the hilltop, with orders to report back to Germany any findings. Mary should be credited for Vallejo's first neighborhood watch!

The Night that Vallejo's Gold Coast Shut Down

Even as the U.S. Government urged its citizens to unite in a common cause, prejudice and discrimination remained an every day reality. Blacks and other people of color were annoyed at this double standard. As Poet Langston Hughes put it, "How long I got to fight - both Hitler and Jim Crow?" (31)

As black Americans intensified their call for equality, white Americans pushed back. Violent confrontations erupted in cities across the U.S., peaking in 1943. In that year, rumors that jobs would go to black workers led thousands of white shipyard employees to burn down black neighborhoods in Beaumont, Texas. In 1943, Detroit, New York City and Los Angeles also experienced large-scale riots.

Vallejo was not immune to such emotions when martial law was declared for about three hours following a race riot in which *"two black sailors were shot and another flare-up was stopped by a cold-nerved police officer." (32)*

Per the Vallejo Times Herald ~ 1942, "The Branciforte-Capitol-Virginia Streets district was the scene of the heaviest activity during the night riot involving black sailors. At least 10 shots were fired by Marines called out on riot duty.

A platoon of Marines and the entire police department were called out to take control, but the actual rioting was quelled by shots fired from the Marines.

The action started shortly before 8 p.m. when a group of more than 200 black sailors congregated in the vicinity of Branciforte and Capitol Streets, near a black nightclub.

After considerable milling about, this mob of sailors started out to 'clean up' the bars containing the white sailors along the "gold coast" of lower Georgia Street, reports indicated.

The mob had advanced only part-way towards Virginia Street when the squad of Marines arrived. They immediately ordered the advancing sailors to halt. The sailors kept coming, crying out threats and throwing bottles and bricks. Many of the men were armed with knives, clubs, pipes and broken bottles, all formidable weapons at close quarters.

When the mob of sailors refused to halt, one Marine put his automatic rifle on full automatic and fired four shots at the feet of the advancing men. A few seconds later, another Marine fired three shots from his rifle, and then another fired three rounds over the heads of the advancing mob with his .45 caliber service revolver.

When two sailors fell to the ground wounded, the mob halted. The sailors were quickly rounded up by the Marines and turned over to the Navy shore patrol.

Another riot nearly broke out at the intersection of Sonoma and Georgia Streets, between two groups of soldiers and sailors, when a black sailor was suspected of pulling a knife on a soldier. The sailor's actions were quickly squelched when five Marines arrived with weapons drawn, and the sailors were led away at gunpoint to join the others already under arrest. All military personnel were ordered to return to the base immediately.

Subsequently, three large navy yard trucks responded to transport the sailors in custody back to the base. There were so many - about 400 sailors in all, that they all couldn't fit into the trucks. Tension was high for more than two hours as the Marines loaded up the sailors into the trucks. Many of the sailors were heard yelling threats and obscenities at the Marines and Navy shore patrol. With each truck carrying about a hundred men each, the remaining 100 sailors were marched back to the base under armed guard.

Armed civilian and military guards closed off an area, bounded by Georgia, Santa Clara and Capitol Streets, with the waterfront on the west. All civilian traffic was restricted.

During the course of the round-up, all bars in the above-restricted area were closed, as well as all other places of business.

Orders came directly from Rear Admiral Friedell that all service personnel within a three-mile radius return to their ship or station immediately. Following these orders, shore patrolmen, along with Vallejo police, entered each place of business throughout the city, ordering all servicemen to return to the base."

Thus, within just a few hours, the "gold coast" of lower Georgia Street, as well as the rest of city, was quieter than it had been for years.

The Motor-Pool Monkey

The Boys of Battery C, soon after setting up their battery on the Lewis Ranch, would adopt a small monkey that quickly became Battery C's pet and was given the moniker of the "Motor-Pool Monkey." Unfortunately, it was against official military policy to have pets within the confines of the barracks, so in order to hide their pet from official eyes, the Boys would teach the monkey to go up into the rafters and hide on command. This seemed to work fine until they were given an unannounced visit from their senior officers. To avoid detection, they had the monkey scramble up into the rafters once they saw the arrival of the officer's jeep. Everything seemed to go well during the inspection, except at last moment, the monkey decided it had to go, and relieved itself from above. The inspecting officers weren't very appreciative of their warm greeting, and the monkey was soon discharged back to civilian life. (34)

Bob's Ashes

211th member Bob Carnes was an avid Boston Red Sox fan prior to coming out west to Vallejo. After the war, and up until his death, he remained a loyal and avid fan of the Red Sox. Upon his death, his sons Kevin and Chris, wanting to honor his legacy as a true fan of the team, paid a visit to Fenway Park. They purchased a brick engraved with Bob's name, and laid it on the park grounds. Later they would return, this time carrying Bob's ashes with them. Some time during the game, when no one was looking, they discreetly spread Bob's ashes under the infamous "Green Monster." So from that point on, Bob Carnes would always have a front row seat to all future games at the park he loved so much.

Recycling in Vallejo

Recycling in Vallejo during World War II became a major cause supported by most locals. The need for rubber was especially important. So important, that the local theaters offered free admission with the donation of a rubber item. As reported by Edie Baker, who was a young woman at the time, one of the kids in her neighborhood, somehow got hold of a huge tractor-size tire. He proceeded to go around the neighborhood, announcing to all his friends, that today's matinee was on him. He and his friends, a dozen strong, rolled the old tire down to the Hanlin Theater on Virginia Street, and sure enough, were all given free admission. It was definitely a "good year" for the boys.

Ray Sherman
In 1989, 211th drummer Ray Sherman was designated "Jazzman of the Year" by Los Angeles' Jazz Forum. During the 1980's, Ray also became interested in writing non-fiction and poetry. His work has been published in *The Humanist* and *Orion* magazines and the British publication, *Jazz Journal*.

The Army Truck
Johnny Walsh remembers very little about his accident in 1943, since he was only 9 years old when it happened, but recalls the tale told to him years later by his mom. *"My mom had gone by bus to Long Beach to visit with my dad whose ship had come into port, but he couldn't leave. Mrs. Andrews, a friend of mom's, stayed with us kids. We all knew her well, as she occasionally stayed with us for short periods of time. I left from home, 106 B Street, on my bicycle traveling down Benson Avenue to Wilson Avenue. As I crossed Wilson, an army vehicle - which I was later told was a reconnaissance car - was passing another vehicle heading north on the two-lane road. The army vehicle was*

in the southbound lane where I was after the crossing, and hit me, knocking me off my bike, of course, and knocking me out as well. I was unconscious, and taken to Vallejo General Hospital, where I spent a day or two, until being transferred to Mare Island Hospital. I had sustained a fractured hip. I was at Mare Island for a few days, and released to my mother for home care. I believe I was taken by ambulance and put in bed at 106, where I remained for about 3 weeks. Mom always said that when I returned to school the first day, we had a spelling test and the only word I missed was "absence." Mom referred to the perp vehicle as "an army truck." That's my story and I'm sticking to it!"

The Boys of Battery D

Battery D was located in the hills overlooking the entrance to Mare Island, the Carquinez Bridge, and the city of Vallejo. Their location was vital since they had a clear vision of the Marin headlands to the west. It was assumed that if further Japanese planes were to attack Mare Island, they would approach from those western hills. Their primary mission, though, was the overview and protection of the Carquinez Bridge. They would set up a battery with a

90mm cannon on the Valona Hill, overlooking the town and the bridge below. Another gun pad was located on the east end of the bridge, just below on the hillside approaching Vallejo. The Boys were also located at the bridgehead, stopping all traffic for inspection.

Battery D's headquarters was set up in the Crockett Striped Bass Club. Like Vallejo across the bridge, the Crockett community would soon reach out to the Boys, providing them with many comfort items, such as blankets, mattresses, toiletries, and countless other items to help their stay be a little more tolerable.

In an open letter to the citizens of Crockett, the commanding officer of Battery D, First Lieutenant Wilbur Powers, would write, *"The officers and men of Battery D, 211th Coast Artillery, First Corps of Cadets, extend their heartfelt thanks and unbounded appreciation for the unstinted cooperation and extreme generosity shown them by the people who live and work in Crockett."*

Lieutenant Powers would go on to write, "All that has been said and written about southern hospitality to us misses the mark. Henceforth, it is West Coast and specifically, Crockett hospitality, that we will always remember and acclaim."

The hospitality of the citizens of Crockett and Vallejo, like that of the entire Bay
Area, was reflective of the patriotism being exhibited by the entire country during this time.

Valentine's Day 1943

The weekend of February 14, 1943 was a busy, but romantic time for at least six of the Boys, who chose that date to marry their sweethearts. All the nuptials were held in Vallejo at various locations, but the first to walk down the aisle that day was Corporal Maurice Godfrey and his bride, Miss Marian Wenstrum. Both from the Boston area, they got married at the Presbyterian Church on Nebraska Street, and were planning to settle in the Vallejo area after the war.

Following their wedding reception, Corporal Godfrey took his bride into San Francisco to one of the nicer hotels, but was greeted with the news that no rooms were available at that time. Corporal Godfrey was quite befuddled, but when the hotel located their application on file, were quick to offer the newlyweds their biggest and best penthouse-wedding suite... on the house, and even threw in a bottle of champagne. Again, just another great example of western hospitality!

Lady Luck

A murder tale that could have come from a Hollywood movie script, tells the story of a 23-year-old Army private, apparently crazed with jealousy and using a borrowed .45 service pistol from his commanding officer, who shot and killed his fiancée. The murder took place inside a local bar in downtown Vallejo on the evening of September 24, 1942. The bar's name was "Lucky's Place."

The private, identified as Romeo d'Aloisio and assigned to the 211th Coastal AA, admitted upon his arrest, to shooting his fiancée, Annette Tipton, after a bitter argument outside the bar.

The case, which would run over six months and be filled with delays and surprises, was covered on the front page of every paper in the county.

D'Aloisio had met Tipton earlier in the year one evening when he and a few of his 211th buddies were hanging out at the Casa de Vallejo Hotel bar, when Tipton approached their table and asked if she could join their party. Being the pretty blond that she was, the Boys were quick to accommodate her request and pulled up an extra chair. She came across as very friendly and, soon after introducing herself, asked for a drink. D'Aloisio was the first to oblige and then asked her to dance. After an hour of drinking and dancing, they were seen walking out of the bar 'arm in arm' with d'Aloisio giving the 'thumbs up' to his buddies.

D'Aloisio and Tipton would continue to see each other over the next several months, with d'Aloisio telling his buddies how he very much liked her, and felt that she was special and thought that "she was the one."

It wasn't soon after, on one of their dates, that Tipton shared with d'Aloisio that she was actually married but getting a divorce, and that he shouldn't worry about continuing to see her. She failed to tell him that she also had a seven year-old daughter, who was apparently living with her husband at another residence.

Tipton who was from Richmond, California often visited the local Vallejo bars during the evening hours. She would tell d'Aloisio that she felt sorry for the young GI's, far from home with no one to talk to.

Their relationship continued to grow, as they saw more and more of each other. On multiple occasions, d'Aloisio would travel to visit Tipton on the promise that she'd be home, only to find her gone. On one occasion, upon knocking on her door, he discovered her home with another man.

D'Aloisio would become agitated with Tipton's behavior and broke down one evening during a visit, telling her how much he loved her, and pleading with her to stop seeing these other men. He was insistent that she move to Vallejo, offered to find her an apartment and to pay her rent just to keep her close.

Tipton suggested that maybe they needed to get away and asked d'Aloisio if he could get a long weekend pass, so they could have a weekend alone together. D'Aloisio liked the idea, but wasn't sure he would be able to get the time off or if he had the money for such a trip. Tipton suggested that he borrow it from someone, maybe his parents or friends. She suggested that it would be a great time for the two of them to talk about their future together, as in getting married. She told him the divorce would be final any day, and that she was looking forward to moving on with him.

D'Aloisio was thrilled to share the announcement of his future engagement with his buddies back at the barracks. Many of them spoke of their concern with him rushing into things, suggesting that maybe he reconsider the engagement. He said he wouldn't think of changing his plans.

The next weekend, d'Aloisio and Annette Tipton would spend three days together in San Francisco, where he formally proposed to Mrs. Tipton, and she graciously accepted.

It was during the moving process the following weekend that d'Aloisio would finally meet Bill Tipton, Annette's husband. Mrs. Tipton had asked him to help in the move. D'Aloisio would drive back to Vallejo by himself to meet Mrs. Tipton and her husband at the Vallejo address after helping with the loading of her possessions.

Upon her own arrival to Vallejo, Mrs. Tipton would introduce Bill to her landlord as her 'brother-in-law', and d'Aloisio as her 'fiancée.' It was after the unloading of Mrs. Tipton's possessions that Bill Tipton pulled d'Aloisio aside and asked him to stop seeing his wife.

By this time, d'Aloisio was becoming frustrated with the relationship, and was starting to argue more with Mrs. Tipton. He appeared depressed and talked to his buddies about how he needed to fix things. D'Aloisio said he really liked her, but she was starting to cost him a lot of money, and he didn't like the idea of her husband being around. He also didn't like the idea that she continued to live in Bill's home during the week, not using the Vallejo room, except on occasions during the weekend.

On the night of the shooting, Annette Tipton and her sister, Coy Estes, arranged to meet d'Aloisio and some of his friends at the Veteran's Memorial Hall in Vallejo. The hall had become a popular place for the soldiers to hang out since it often would have dances with live music. D'Aloisio had arrived with other soldiers from headquarters, including Lieutenant Colonel Francis Beaver, Superior Officer of d'Aloisio. It was never made clear to investigators later as to how or why, but d'Aloisio apparently took possession of Colonel Beaver's weapon, a .45 service pistol, under the auspice of cleaning the weapon for him. While doing so, he received a phone call from Mrs. Tipton to tell him that she was going to go visit a couple of bars, but would send her sister to pick him up and they could meet up later at Lucky's. In d'Aloisio's frustration and haste, he put the pistol into his service jacket pocket and headed out of the building.

Tipton's sister, Miss Estes, would testify later that she did indeed pick up d'Aloisio in front of the Veteran's Hall, and did drive him to the bar. She stated that they parked across the street from Lucky's, and she then went inside to get her sister. She stated that when Tipton came out and approached the car, d'Aloisio pulled out his pistol, and holding it against her sister's head, forced her into the alley. There, Miss Estes said, d'Aloisio threatened to kill Tipton if she tried to escape.

D'Aloisio would later testify that he just wanted to make things right, but Tipton kept screaming at him, saying she wished he were dead. He stated that he handed the pistol to her, asking her to kill him. He stated that she fired two rounds at him, but missed, dropped the gun and then dashed into what she thought was the safety of Lucky's. Picking up the weapon, d'Aloisio followed her into the bar and fired six rounds at her point blank as she stood at the bar.

Tipton was already dead when Inspector Ralph Jenson and Sergeant Dan Horan arrived to investigate. The investigators found her body sprawled on the floor of the tavern.

Lucky's Place

The arresting officers testified that d'Aloisio admitted to shooting her four or five times and stating, *"She was no good. She was just a tramp and took me for everything I had."* The officers stated later that d'Aloisio then asked them what kind of capital punishment they had in California and said he hoped it was not the electric chair.

At the Vallejo police station, d'Aloisio was booked and jailed on murder charges. The post mortem report from Coroner Gertrude Klotz revealed that five bullets from a .45 semi-automatic had entered Tipton's body.

Klotz identified the shot that killed Tipton as a back shot that entered the heart.

From the evening of the arrest to the first day of the juried trial, several months would pass, brought on by delays, continuances, and requests for withdraws from councel by the defendant's attorney. The original complaint filed in the Police Court of the City of Vallejo on September 25, 1942 against Romeo d'Aloisio read: Romeo d'Aloisio did willfully and unlawfully and feloniously, and with malice aforethought, murder one Annette Tipton, a human being. Judge V.M. Castagnetto, Police Chief Earl Dierking and Attorney John Bradley signed the complaint. Romeo d'Aloisio would plead his innocence.

Attorney Phillip Lynch was assigned as the prosecuting attorney representing the state. Attorney Lynch stated that he would seek the death penalty. Attorney Ellis Randall would be assigned the task of defending d'Aloisio and Lt. Phillip Lawrence would serve as U.S. Army Legal Council.

The first twist in the case happened when Judge V.M. Castagnetto requested that he be disqualified from the case on the grounds that he was a member of the law firm of O'Hara, Randall, and Castagnetto, of which the defense attorney Randall Ellis was also a member. Judge Castagnetto would eventually be replaced by Judge W.T.O'Donnell who would end up presiding over the rest of the case.

The next delay surfaced when defense attorney Ellis moved that he be allowed to withdraw as counsel to the defendant. Attorney Ellis stated that due to the seriousness of the charge against d'Aloisio, a private in the Army, and the fact that he [Ellis] was about to enter into the service of the United States Naval Reserve and would require extra time to prepare for this entry into the service, didn't feel he could provide the counsel required by d'Aloisio. The court approved his movement and the trial was postponed until December 15.

The first day of the trial would end with a venire of 95 prospective jurors being exhausted and 11 women in the jury box. As the court closed for the day, the prosecution had made use of four of its peremptory challenges in excusing persons from service, and the defense 13 of its 20 peremptory challenges.

A special venire of 30 prospective jurors was summoned to complete the jury. The defense, according to all indications, was attempting to obtain an all-women jury. Finally, the next day, the jury panel was finally filled with the selection of its last member, a male.

The defense would have eleven soldiers, from a lieutenant colonel to a private, testify that Romeo d'Aloisio was unable to rid himself of a "fatal attraction" exercised over him by Mrs. Annette Tipton, and that he was brooding and despondent over their relationship and aborted marriage plans before he shot her to death the night of September 24, 1942.

The soldiers and civilian witnesses were called in a daylong parade to the witness stand, all building testimony on the relationship between the girl and the soldier who later killed her.

From the line of questioning on the part of the defense, it appeared that they were driving at a dual purpose:

1. That d'Aloisio was driven to his crime by unrequited love for Mrs. Tipton, that he was disillusioned and bitter when he found out she was married and not free to wed him, and that he was angered that she broke dates with him to go out with others.
2. That because of his reputation for "truth, honesty, and integrity," the jury could take his word as the unbiased truth when he goes on the witness stand to defend himself.

The Solano County Superior Court jury would acquit Romeo d'Aloisio of a charge of murder and did not deliberate on any of the three murder counts. Instead, the jury confined their deliberation to manslaughter or acquittal. His possession of the gun, the jury felt, was accidental, based on the defense testimony of the witness who testified he saw d'Aloisio slip the weapon he was cleaning on orders of his commanding officer, into his inside pocket when he was summoned to the telephone call from Mrs. Tipton.

In the jury's mind, there was no doubt that the soldier killed Mrs. Tipton. But in the jury's mind, d'Aloisio showed "no malice of forethought" or he would have killed her when they were sitting in the car in the alley, when he was allegedly pleading with her, and according to his testimony, Tipton fired the gun twice at him when he suggested she "blow his brains out." Instead, the jury felt d'Aloisio was goaded to the act by several events and "blew his top."

There is a term used by the legal eagles referred to as "jury nullification." Jury nullification occurs when a jury returns a verdict of "Not Guilty" despite its belief that the defendant is guilty of the violation charged. The jury in effect nullifies a law it believes is either immoral or wrongly applied to the defendant whose fate they are charged with deciding.

The country was at war and patriotism was running high. Most of the witnesses for the defense were in Army green uniforms. The jury saw a poor soldier away from home, and while trying to defend their community, was being misled by a woman who intentionally used him for her own personal gain.

Lady Luck simply ran out of her luck at Lucky's Place.

Returning Home

Colonel Stuart G. Hall and Captain Donald R. MacDonald, both were killed in an air crash as they flew via Army transporter from San Francisco to Hamilton Field. Their plane crashed into the San Pablo Bay. All seven soldiers on board were killed.

Colonel Hall, 51, was the Commanding Officer of the 211th Coastal Anti-Aircraft Artillery Regiment. He led the regiment west into Vallejo, and maintained command until his transfer to Army headquarters in San Francisco.

Captain MacDonald, 26, a member of Colonel Hall's staff, came to Vallejo as an enlisted man with the 211th and remained in Vallejo until his appointment to Officers'

Candidate School in December 1943. He was engaged to Vallejoan Alyce Tregaskis at the time of his death.

Their remains were returned to their Massachusetts homes for military funerals with full honors.

CHAPTER 15

The Boys

VALLEJO TIMES HERALD Editor Wyman Riley reported in his October, 1962 Sunday Notebook column that, *"There probably is no community in the United States so affected by troops stationed within its city than Vallejo."*

In his column, he listed some of the names of the Boys who had returned to the City of Vallejo after the war, and the occupations and professions they held within the community.

*W. Akkerman - Real Estate Sales
*Bill Babbitt - Photography
*John Barkas - State Board of Equalization
*Jim Barlow - Retail Food & Beverage
*Mario Barrasso - C&H Sugar
*Matt Baxley - Pacific Telephone
*Brigadier General Frank Beaver - US Army
*Col. Veto Blekaitis - US Army
*Paul Bogosian - Barber
*Phil Bourgeious - Department of Motor
  Vehicles
*Ed Burns - Retail Food & Beverage

*Raymond Carey - C&H Sugar
*Bob Carnes - Printer
*Eldon Cecil - Transportation
*Harry Clark - Labor Representative
*Tom Coleman - Retail Food & Beverage
*Leo Cullen - Pacific Telephone
*Tom Cullen - Mare Island
*Paul Davenport - Medical Sales
*Jim Davis - Fire Department
*Dick Debrun - Transportation
*Wes Defoe - Pacific Gas & Electric
*John DeMello - Hardware and Paint
*Sgt. Joe DeMello - US Army
*Roger Dempsey -Pacific Gas & Electric
*Louis DePass - Radio & Television
*Art Di Sangro - Food & Beverage
*Denny Dwyer - Mare Island
*Jack Dumphy - Mare Island
*Jack East - Pacific Gas & Electric
*Ken Eckland - Auto Repair
*Vince Ellis - Mare Island
*Bill Fein - Transportation
*Tony Ferris - Mare Island
*Lieutenant Colonel Bob Fiske - US Army
*Al Franzosa - Auto Repair
*Dom Gervasi - Pacific Telephone
*Dugald Gillies - Newspaper Columnist
*Red Graham - Banker
*Captain William Hanley - US Army
*Paul Harding - Mare Island
*Richard Hunt - Hercules Power

*Bob Kukuruza - Auto Tow Service
*Charlie Landry - Mare Island
*Ed Lawson - Banker
*Jim Lear - Food & Beverage
*George Madden - Mare Island
*James Madison - C&H Sugar
*Joe Malloch - C&H Sugar
*Barney Martin - Food & Beverage
*Bob Martin - Food & Beverage
*Harvey McInerney - Food & Beverage
*Joe McNamara - Post Office
*Art Medeiros - Electrician
*Pat Medeiros - Auto Repair
*Fred Meggers - US Merchant Marine
*Bob Metcalf - Pacific Gas & Electric
*Chick Miller - Fire Department
*Tom Mitchell - Registered Nurse
*Ed Morrell - Pacific Telephone
*Bob Narcisci - Barber
*Joe Nickerson -Pacific Gas & Electric
*Sergeant Bud Nolan - US Army
*Ed Noonan - Title Search
*Vince Pace
*John Page - Publications
*Lieutenant Colonel James Peck - US Army
*Art Pelaquin - US Government
*Bill Pendergast - Auto Repair
*Clayton Philbrook -Mare Island
*Colonel George Powers - US Army
*John Quinn
*Al Robinson -Mare Island

*Jack Roche - Fire Department
*Carmin Rollins - Court Reporter
*Ed Rollins - Mare Island
*Ed Rowell - Pacific Telephone
*Robert Rubin - Banker
*Jim Sanderson - Mare Island
*Victor Santos
*Henry Schultz - Sales
*Frank Smith - Mare Island
*Al Stackenburg - C&H Sugar
*Bob Staples - Pacific Telephone
*Bill Sutton - Pacific Gas & Electric
*Bill Tedesco - Mare Island
*Charles Tisdale - Food & Beverage
*Joe Toronto - Music Sales/Cleaners
*Bob Wade - Public Relations
*Bill Ward - Law Enforcement
*Captain Tom Wilson - US Army
*Slim Winberg - Advertising
*Joe White - Law Enforcement

CHAPTER 16

Moments

As a child I have memories of my father showing me pictures of his extended family back in Boston. He spoke often of having several aunts and lots of cousins.

Pictures of his Boston family were always on display and he always had a camera in his hand when I was a kid. It was those pictures, those 'connections' that he had captured, which reinforced those memories to this day.

In preparing to write this story about the Boys, I collected and reviewed hundreds of pictures saved over the years, either by my father or from the other 211th families, and in doing so, I tried to visualize them in the same way, their moments, trying to bring them closer and, thus, giving me an easier understanding of the story they told.

My father had two blood brothers. My Uncle Tom came west with my dad on those trains from Texas.

Like my dad, he, too, would return to Vallejo after the war. My other uncle, their much younger brother, Paul, was too young at the time to enlist in the Army, but not wanting to be left out, would later enlist at the first opportunity, into the U.S. Marines. Unfortunately, he was killed in action during the Korean conflict at the young age of 22. I never had an opportunity to meet him, but again, due to those pictures of old, I can envision my uncle very clearly.

My father went on to serve in the Asiatic Pacific Campaign, being deployed to New Guinea, and later, to the Philippines, while my Uncle Tom eventually served in the European Campaign. My father and uncle, upon their discharges, would eventually join the hundreds of Boys who returned to the area after the war.

As I grew older, I later realized who those other Boys were, and the significance of their relationships with each other. They represented my father's other Boston brothers. Weekends would arrive, and my father would bring me with him when he visited these brothers. What I thought was just 'getting some gas for the car' as he would tell my mom, would turn into a visit to Bill Pendergast's service station. It always turned into an hour-long visit.

Then we would drop by Joe Toronto's Sparkle Cleaners on Tennessee Street, supposedly to pick up our laundry, but that, too, would turn into a 30- minute visit. Same with visits to John De Mello's paint store or Bob Kukuruza's auto yard. The Boys liked to visit each other and talk.

My father and mother had three of the Boys in their wedding. My godparents were Bob and Mary Carnes. Bob served with 211th AA Regimental Band. I believe my parents returned the favor for one of their many offspring. These kinds of favors were widespread among the Boys and their families. Over the years, they would celebrate and honor the birthdays, anniversaries, and the passing of one of their brothers.

This special bond was reinforced every five years after the war with the on-going reunions. The Boys were proud to have served their country, and to have discovered Vallejo in the process. Strangers at the beginning, they became brothers at the end.

———

Research for this story required the help of many. Local citizens, all young at heart, contributed their memories of what it was like to live in Vallejo during the war.

Thank you to the following 211th families who contributed in my research: Akkermann, Carey, Carnes, Christo, Davis, De Mello, Di Sangro, Dwyer, Eckland, Graves, Kukuruza, Madison, Martin, Mayes, McInerney, Medeiros, Mellock, Pendergast, Robinson, C.Rollins, E. Rollins, Tedesco, Sherman, Tisdale and Toronto.

My gratitude goes to the 211th wives who graciously allowed me into their homes and shared their stories: Ada, Alma, Celeste, Desiree, Dorothy, Rose, Teddy and Ursula.

Special thanks need to go to John De Mello. He is the lone Vallejo surviving 211th member, with whom I was fortunate to have spent hours in doing my research. I loved listening to his stories of the old days back in Boston and their travels west. John, who served in Battery G, was proud of the fact that his group was the last of the Boys to leave Vallejo.

I also need to acknowledge the work of Brendan Riley and Jim Kern for their official editing of my drafts, and Doug Keener for his legal-ease offerings.

Before I finish, I need to acknowledge my wife and angel, Teri, who patiently sat through my moments of wavering, navigated over and around my piles of research, delicately redirected me through my grammatical and spelling miscues and gave me strength at times when I wasn't able to formulate a real thought.

To finish, I need to thank my father. His spirit was the driving force for me to record this story - a story based on actual events, a story that needed to be told. Thanks dad for those 'connections.'

SSGt. Leo James Cullen

Bibliography

1. Leonid Kondratiuk, Monstrat Viam: A History of the 211th Military Police Battalion (First Corps of Cadets). Washington, Historical Services Branch, National Guard Bureau, April 1997, 10pp.

   (Revised and corrected October 2009 for publication here by C. Brown, First Corps of Cadets Museum Boston)

2. The Boston Irish: A Political History Thomas H. O'Connor, 1995

3. Boston News Source

4. ibid

5. ibid

6. ibid

7. Matagorda County Historical Commission, Historic Matagorda County (3 vols. Houston: Armstrong, 1986). Ruby Penland, Camp Hulen, Texas (Palacios, Texas: Palacios Area Historical Association, 1987).

8. Cressman, Robert J. (2000). The Official Chronology of the U.S. Navy in World War

II. Annapolis, Maryland: Naval Institute Press.

9. How Trains Helped Win a War: Richard C. Roberts Beehive History - Utah History to Go.

10. "A giant cannon aimed at the Pacific." National Park Service's WWII ~ In the San Francisco Bay Area~Golden Gate National Recreation Area

11. ibid

12. Chin, Brian B. Artillery at the Golden Gate: The Harbor Defenses of San Francisco in World War II. Missoula, MT: Pictorial Histories Publishing

13. ibid

14. The San Francisco Bay Area Golden Gate National Recreation Area - World War II in the San Francisco Bay Area: produced by the National Park Service's National Register of Historic Places and Golden Gate National Recreation Area, in partnership with the National Trust for Historic Preservation.

15. How Were World War II Searchlights Used: A STORY OF LOCATORS, LIGHTS, & ACK-ACK. World Wide Web (WWW)

16. Aerospace Power Journal - Summer 1989, The Official Web Site of the 225th AAA Searchlight Battalion Veterans Association

17. Johnson, Marilynn S. The Second Gold Rush: Oakland and the East Bay in World War II. Berkeley: University of California Press, 1993.

18. Encyclopedia of Media and Propaganda in Wartime America edited by Martin J. Manning, 17Clarence R. Wyatt

19. ibid

20. ibid

21. Home Front: Economy in WWII; World Wide Web

22. Herman A. Norton, Struggling for Recognition: The United States Army. Chaplaincy, 1791-1865, Washington, D.C.: Government Printing Office, 1977,49; Earl F. Stover, Up from Han&man: The United States Army Chaplaincy 1865-1920,

Washington, D.C., Government Printing Office, 1977,

23. All Music: Biography by Scott Yanow

24. Wynn, Ron. "Ray Bauduc: Biography". All Music. Retrieved 21 August 2011.

25. The Musicians: A Chronicle of Vallejo's Bands 1920-1949

26. ibid

27. ibid

28. Vallejo Times Herald 6/13/1943

29. The Musicians: A Chronicle of Vallejo's Bands 1920-1949

30. Yale-New Haven Teachers Institute ((Langston Hughes: Artist and Historian) by Medria Blue

31. Vallejo Times Herald, 1942

32. ibid

33. Crockett And Its People (1981) David A. Billec

Made in the USA
San Bernardino, CA
06 February 2016